THE
WILD
LAND
WITHIN

Praise for
THE WILD LAND WITHIN

"It's easy to get lost in a dense wood or a big city. But it's even easier to get lost in the tangles of our inner lives. In this book, Lisa Colón DeLay offers some of the best inner-life guidance I know. Drawing on the many sound sources she's studied with care, including her own experience, she shares time-tested wisdom for people seeking a spiritual GPS to keep them oriented to true self. Highly recommended."

—Parker J. Palmer, author of *On the Brink of Everything; A Hidden Wholeness; Let Your Life Speak;* and *The Courage to Teach*

"Lisa Colón DeLay is a thoughtful, discerning, and encouraging guide to *The Wild Land Within*—an 'ecosystem of grace,' a sacred place in our hearts and souls where we encounter the Divine Presence and learn to bear the beams of love. To read this book is to embark on a transformational spiritual adventure."

—Carl McColman, author of *Eternal Heart* and other books

"Every single page of this book pushes you to explore every aspect of your inner life and gaze upon a God who is able to provide peace and grow you despite what you may find. After reading this book, you'll never look at spiritual growth books the same."

—Terence Lester, founder of Love Beyond Walls

"Lisa Colón DeLay is a spiritual cartographer. She maps out the lay of our spiritual land utilizing scripture, experience, and the Christian wisdom tradition throughout the ages, along with reason and psychology. . . . This is a wise, robust debut from an experienced spiritual director. It is a much-needed contribution to spiritual formation by a Latina woman in the Protestant world. I am incredibly thankful for it."

—Marlena Graves, author of *The Way Up Is Down*

"The climatological and geological metaphors in this book were powerful for me. Chasms, fire, still water, wildness—all plunged me more deeply into confronting myself and God in those places I don't often confront or talk about. I was blessed by the dangerous adventure of *The Wild Land Within*."

—Jon M. Sweeney, author of *The Pope Who Quit* and other books

"Lisa Colón DeLay is your companion and guide through the landscape of the interior. It is a wonderful journey that not only brings us closer to ourselves, but also helps us engage with our world and communities. . . . During these times of uncertainty, hardships, and even trauma, *The Wild Land Within* provides a roadmap for navigating the aching of the heart and soul, the yearnings of the mind and body."

—Phuc Luu, author of *Jesus of the East*

"Lisa Colón DeLay offers a hearty, thoughtful, and thorough approach to navigating the terrain of our spiritual lives. From Quakers to cognitive development, from desert fathers to twentieth-century priests and poets, she details the true journey we humans undertake with God. This book is a gift to the conversation around spiritual transformation in Christ."

—Casey Tygrett, author of *As I Recall*

"In these pages, Lisa Colón DeLay charts a path toward wholeness . . . inviting us to a reintegration through the diligent inner work of contemplative prayer and attentive listening to the wisdom of the forgotten and marginalized, from Evagrius Ponticus to African American and Latinx spirituality. In her writing and guidance through the inner terrain, Lisa bears the marks of genuine transformation from wound to love. This is profoundly insightful, important, and illuminating work."

—Marc Thomas Shaw, executive director of Contemplative Light

"Lisa Colón DeLay is a cartographer of the soul. Having ventured through its hills, forests, and ravines, she knows where the hidden creatures lurk and how to cut a path through its darker regions. The result is *The Wild Land Within*, a spiritual map for reconnecting head and heart, thought and feeling, desire and action. Thoughtful, practical, and delightfully written, this is an enriching book that can help us become whole."

—Sheridan Voysey, author of *The Making of Us* and other books

THE
WILD
LAND
WITHIN

Cultivating Wholeness
through Spiritual Practice

LISA COLÓN DeLAY

BROADLEAF BOOKS
MINNEAPOLIS

THE WILD LAND WITHIN
Cultivating Wholeness through Spiritual Practice

Cover image: saemilee/istock
Cover design: Lindsey Owens

Print ISBN: 978-1-5064-6508-1
eBook ISBN: 978-1-5064-6509-8

Note: Names and personal details of the people profiled in this book have been altered to protect their privacy.

To my father,
Joseph Robert Colón:
you were such an avid learner and reader,
and you would be overjoyed at this book and
celebrate it with so much gladness and pride.
Thank you for your life and your love.

To my husband, Tim;
my daughter, Gabrielle;
and my son, Nathan,
whose lives I am so grateful for
and whose love keeps me going.

CONTENTS

1

THE WILDS WITHIN

Beginning Our Journey

"Flyover country" is what I saw when I gazed out the window. Traveling by air from Chicago to San Francisco, I was fascinated by how little I knew of these landscapes. Down below, thousands of square miles of beautiful fields in Iowa and Nebraska stretched out like a patchwork. The stark wilderness landscapes of Colorado featured thick forests and high mountains—the highest were capped with snow. Over Utah were expanses of barren salt flats. Then there was Nevada, with miles of uninhabited rugged desert terrains, canyons, and cliffs. And there was Lake Tahoe, fed by the streams coming from the verdant mountains of the Sierra Nevada. As a resident of the East Coast, I realized how unlikely it was that I would ever venture into those wild places.

My inner world has unknown terrain, and so does yours. This expanse includes our minds, hearts, wills, and spirits. The wild land within also includes our experiences, aspirations, and memories. And like it or not, this territory also includes shadowy areas of hidden influencers as well as triggering thoughts and feelings.

For many of us, the wild land within remains unexplored territory that we seldom navigate. We hardly know anything about it. We all, at times, avoid looking at painful or difficult parts of our inner selves because of our fears or the commotion of our lives. Some people manage to avert their gaze from their interior terrains for a lifetime.

The Wild Land Within is an invitation to explore your own flyover country. This book serves as a companion to search the inner and unseen but very real territory of yourself. As we attend to this land within, our journey will involve some issues you may know little or nothing about. There are places of rough and even terrifying terrain. We will learn what makes spiritual growth unnecessarily difficult or extra confusing. To explore this land within means encountering climate and storms, negotiating treacherous topography, and finding creatures both wounded and wild.

This book will introduce you to the wide array of internal landscapes that include those inconvenient, uncomfortable, and wild spots too many spiritual or religious types pretend aren't there. Your inner landscape is a world worthy of investigation and familiarity. This exploration will be unlike any other you've done so far. My hope is that you discover healing and wholeness during this journey and renewed intimacy with the Lover of your Soul.

When Spiritual Practices Don't Work

You may be coming to this book with confusion, frustration, or anxiety. You may be feeling stuck in a spiritual, occupational, or relational rut. You may be wondering why reading the Bible doesn't make you feel closer to God or why praying sometimes makes you feel *more* alone. Despite all you may have heard about a life of abundant joy, these feelings of distance from God are not uncommon aspects of the spiritual journey.

Perhaps you've been wondering why spiritual practices don't seem to "work" for you. Perhaps you've been wondering why it's hard to quiet down and pray—why when you start to get still, your mind starts bouncing like a little tree full of rowdy monkeys. Or maybe you've noticed that anxiety or restlessness plays a bigger part in your life than you want them to as you try to concentrate on reading Scripture. It can be confusing because the spiritual habits that are supposed to bring us peace—such as journaling, silent retreat, fasting, meditation, or devotional reading—can sometimes bring anger or pain to the surface instead. If that is your experience, then you've found the right book. I had you in mind as I wrote this.

You are not alone. In my experience as a spiritual companion—in the Celtic tradition, it's called an *anam cara*, or "soul friend"—I've listened to people as they have struggled with spiritual drought, sadness, loneliness, and anxiety. Too often they have felt abnormal for having what are actually common human experiences. In my listening ministry, it is not uncommon for people to tell me that trying out new (to them) spiritual practices sometimes has left them feeling more confused, upset, or alienated than before they began. The same things have happened to me as well. This is why spiritual companionship is so important.

Feeling like a misfit—or "out of joint"—during the spiritual formation process is not a strange or unique affliction. It's part of being human and maturing in faith. Instead of languishing and feeling isolated from God, others, and even the deepest parts of ourselves, we can journey together on a path not around but *through* the wilderness. We will discover our inner terrains and become braver travelers within the next chapters.

For many years, my main work and passions have focused on spiritual formation. It involves how we heal and grow. I have worked as a writer and as the host of the *Spark My Muse* podcast, broadcasting episodes on spiritual topics every single week since April 2015 and interviewing scores of people who have traveled the wild land within and who help others find their way too. As a teacher, I have guided federal prison inmates, taught educators at the graduate level, and hosted retreats on the Bible, contemplative prayer, and devotional practices. And I've walked with others in spiritual friendship over the course of decades. Through it all, I've sensed Divine Love calling me, and calling out through me, to invite others to a deeper embrace of grace. There is healing available through growing in intimacy with the Divine Love—who may perhaps be a little different than the kind of God that you heard about growing up. Being a student of Jesus is a lifelong apprenticeship, not just a series of services to attend or beliefs to learn. This apprenticeship is also an ongoing, intimate communion with the Living One. It is a lifestyle that trains us in loving others—and ourselves.

Too many times our spiritual lives become siloed into aspects of behavior modification or trying hard to be nicer. Real, lasting transformation doesn't happen through these efforts. Some of us find this out the hard way, and we arrive exhausted at a place of burnout. Transformation must involve root-level, inner discovery and deep spiritual and personal shifts that lead to life anew. This is how we grow to be resilient in all the circumstances of life and can begin to give, in service to others, out of an overflowing of love.

Choosing Our Guides

The wild land within is not a place to journey alone. When we travel to unknown places, wise guides are essential. In these pages, we will have help along the way. For insights on spiritual formation and healing, we will enlist the help of some modern contemplative and spiritual teachers. These escorts, who often rely on ancient Christian spiritual practices, include Parker J. Palmer, Henri Nouwen, Cynthia Bourgeault, Dallas Willard, John O'Donohue, Lerita Coleman Brown, Carl McColman, Thomas Merton, Angela Tilby, Thomas Keating, Mary Mrozowski, Howard Thurman, and others. For understanding the workings of our brains and emotions, we will turn to experts in neuroscience and therapy such as Dr. Bessel A. van der Kolk, therapist Liz Mullinar, Dr. Lisa Feldman Barrett, and Dr. Joseph LeDoux. For understanding the besetting issues in our inner lives, we will enlist the wise voices of the early monastic and Eastern church elders like Anthony of Egypt (251–376 CE) and Evagrius Ponticus (345–400 CE). These guides spent much of their lives praying in the literal wilderness—in desert solitude—and helping spiritual seekers who sought their guidance.

My perspective might be a little different than yours. As a mixed-ethnicity, Latinx woman born in Puerto Rico, I was surrounded by people of color. The first world I knew—this small American island territory, roughly the size of Connecticut, in the Caribbean Sea—was not white-centered or white-dominated. When my family later settled in the mainland United States, I was a bilingual young girl who had to adapt to white-centered surroundings and white-dominated schools and institutions. Being light-skinned, I passed as white, and I usually didn't suffer abuse the way nonwhite people would. But my father and other family members with dark skin or Spanish accents were routinely singled out, ridiculed, marginalized, or worse. I soon realized that on the US mainland, certain people were in control and experienced preferential treatment. In graduate school, I attended a white-centered, largely male-dominated seminary. I realized that space was governed by a distinct few as well. Only rarely was I introduced to professors, teachings, and books authored by those who were unlike the people who founded the school—educated, moneyed, white, and male. The curriculum and surroundings demonstrated to me that these perspectives and voices were granted the most respect, authority, and value in that environment. My life experiences taught me, sometimes painfully, that when we fail to learn from our brothers and sisters who have been marginalized and minoritized—the "least of these" Jesus speaks of in the beatitudes—we are all worse for it. I share pieces of my journey with you in the coming pages so it may add uniquely to your spiritual formation.

That distinction might make this book unlike most other books that you have encountered about spiritual formation. Unfortunately, few books on the spiritual life and contemplative practice feature the theological input, wisdom, and perspectives of Black, Indigenous, Latinx, and people of color (BILPOC). The acronym *BILPOC* refers to Americans of African descent, Native American and Indigenous people, Latinx (Latina/o), and other persons who appear to be nonwhite. Let's be truthful: light-skinned people of Western European heritage presume preeminence in cultural conversations in the United States and other places in the world. This presumption is usually an unconscious one. We live in a robust culture of plurals, and when BILPOC voices stay marginalized, the entire society is poorer for it and all perspectives become distorted. When we do not value historically subjugated voices and make them part of the mainstream understanding, we get only a warped glimpse of the *Imago Dei*, or the "image of God," within each human.

Within these chapters, we will also look at how the choice of our spiritual guides—those we choose and those we *don't*—deeply affects our spiritual formation. Our growth in Christlikeness depends on our understandings of the people who are often relegated and undervalued. They are shelved and labeled as merely "contextual" spiritualities. The Christian spiritualities of BILPOC contain the good news of the gospel in ways people of an affluent, dominant culture may be uncomfortable or unfamiliar with. This book will attempt to disrupt common presumptions of white-centeredness that often remain unchallenged and unnoticed. For insights into trauma, grief, suffering, and spiritual formation, we will learn from some groups whose spirituality has often been forged in the furnaces of suffering, poverty, oppression, and colonization. These are the lives that echo the experiences of Jesus of Nazareth. Theologians such as Gustavo Gutiérrez, Ada Maria Isasi-Diaz, George Tinker,

James H. Cone, Barbara A. Holmes, Phuc Luu, Wilda Gafney, Fred Shuttlesworth, and others will inform us.

Mapping Our Way

Each chapter in this book will introduce essential insights for understanding the inner life. We will look at histories and contexts that may have exerted hidden influences on our spiritual formation as well as those that may be unfamiliar to us. We will survey the territory of core wounds from childhood, the false identities we develop to protect ourselves, and the shifting weather patterns of temptation to encounter new ways of understanding healing and wholeness. We will learn how trauma and grief uniquely affect our lands within and discern ways to avoid hazards that lead to spiritual malformation. Plus, we will learn how our brains and emotions function in coordination with our physiological responses, and we will become familiar with the wild, vulnerable, and paradoxical parts of our inner worlds.

At the end of each chapter, you will be invited to put into practice an activity for spiritual growth. The suggested spiritual practice might involve answering some questions, reading and reflecting on some text, or learning an enriching kind of prayer. These practices will take you through your land within in richer and deeper ways than you may have expected. This is how we grow. Take time to dig into these sections with the bravery needed and the attentiveness your wild land within deserves.

Try to find at least one reading companion (or a few) to talk about this book as you read it together. You will all be better for it. Additionally, a spiritual mentor, spiritual director, or guide can offer you grounded companionship, perspective, and support as you move through the terrain described in these pages. You can find a resource for that in the back of this book. Because we will be headed into rugged emotional topography, you may find the help of a professional therapist or counselor useful, especially if the material becomes triggering. This book is not a replacement for or an attempt at therapy. When we discuss something that hijacks your emotions, it is wise for you to investigate further, using the skills of a trained practitioner.

Window on Ourselves

The Johari Window is a simple heuristic that can help us understand what we know (and don't know) about ourselves and what others know (and don't know) about us. Developed by psychologists Joseph Luft and Harrington Ingham, the Johari Window has four quadrants that help define our awareness, and others' awareness, of us.

Quadrant 1 represents what we know about ourselves and what others can confirm about us. The other three areas are at

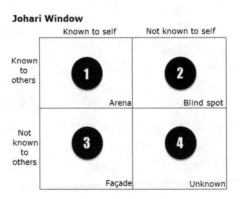

least partially concealed from either ourselves or others. These three quadrants are the primary focus of this book. (Despite the symmetry you see in the model, quadrants of equal shape and size do not exist in real life.)

Quadrant 2 represents all that we do not perceive about ourselves but that *others* notice about us. Understandably, we cannot see a hidden area. When we lack self-awareness or habits of self-reflection, we can have a wide zone of ignorance. Additionally, if we are coping with open wounds or trauma or if we have poor soul-care hygiene, we may be too distracted to be or stay self-aware. When this occurs, our "blind spot" areas get so large that we become more difficult to be around.

We've all known a person who has a large quadrant 2 area, haven't we? People with a large quadrant 2 area are oblivious to the feelings of others. We've all met people who, like petulant children, must have their own way or else they turn on the drama or launch an emotional ice age. Even though they may be complaining about the flaws of others, they will be unaware of how tormenting and infuriating they themselves can be. For those people, we can learn to have a little more compassion because we all have a quadrant 2. In fact, the smaller you think your own quadrant 2 is, the larger it is likely to be. But don't worry, we can reduce the size of our unknown spots by undertaking specific actions: making time and space for self-discovery and knowledge, asking for feedback with a humble and teachable spirit, being open to mentoring and discipleship, and engaging in spiritual practices that nurture mindfulness. All four of these strategies are covered in this book in some form, so keep reading! We are on our way to a smaller quadrant 2.

Quadrant 3 is where we keep our secrets. This is the part of us that remains concealed from others but known to us. From this place, we may use a facade, keep things camouflaged, code switch, or refrain from disclosing information about ourselves and our true feelings. We operate from quadrant 3 for a variety of reasons: when we are insecure, are afraid of being betrayed, feel the need to show off, or are apprehensive of divulging too much. Trauma will make this area larger. If we are concerned about social acceptance, we may engage in posturing or we may withhold words or actions that we think could make others disapprove of us. We may put on displays that we hope will make us more lovable, acceptable, or impressive. Social media seems to have been invented for issues in quadrant 3. We can act like big shots from this quadrant. When we have a secure sense of our true selves, and when we have trusting relationships with others, we can then nurture the relational bonds that cause quadrant 3 to diminish in size. Though all of us need a quadrant 3 to have a semblance of privacy, control, and healthy boundaries, a large quadrant 3 makes for an anxious and bumpy life.

Quadrant 4, which remains unknown to us *and* to others, represents our growing edges. This area of total unknown is reduced when we take on new challenges or responsibilities; seek mentoring, counseling, or therapy; and encounter new situations that contain growth opportunities.

So how can we distinguish when we are making headway into quadrant 4 if it is fully obscured? What is in quadrant 4 is only known after it moves into one of the other quadrants. We will know we are unearthing something from this unknown space when we sense the positive discomfort that comes from being

pushed a bit beyond what we are used to. We've all had stretch-
ing experiences—when we've done what is just beyond what is
known and comfortable. These experiences, both external and
internal, help us see our strengths and weaknesses more clearly.

If we are attentive during those times and reflect as we go
through them or soon after, we can uncover more and more of
the wild land within. We can gently and carefully expose more
and more of this unknown area to the light of our knowledge, of
others' care, and of God's grace and love. For this book to help
you best discover what is in quadrant 4, keep a healthy mix of
apprehension and excitement as we move along and trust in
Divine Love to guide you as more of the land within is revealed.

The Four Soils

Using the metaphor of landscape to represent the inner life is
not a new idea. Jesus spoke directly to the condition of the inner
life when he shared what is known as the four soils parable,
recorded in Matthew 13:1–23, Mark 4:1–20, and Luke 8:4–15.

The allegory of the four soils can be explained this way:
There are four kinds of soil where the sower disperses the
seeds. The sower is the messenger, the seeds represent the message of God, and the soils represent our wild lands within.
First, some seeds fall on a hard-packed type of soil that belongs
to a trampled footpath. They have no chance to grow. Second,
some seeds fall on ground that is rocky beneath the topsoil. The
seeds germinate and grow right away, but the roots cannot go
very deep. When the hot sun of trials and suffering arrives, the
tender plants wither and die. Third are the seeds that fall onto

soil with neighboring weeds and thorns, which correspond to distractions and desires in one's life. They include, in Jesus's words in Mark 4:19 NKJV, "the cares of this world, the deceitfulness of riches, and the desires for other things." The weeds and thorns crowd in and choke the life out of what has sprouted, and these young plants also die.

The fourth and final soil Jesus mentions is the Goldilocks kind: it's *just right.* In good soil, seeds germinate, grow deep roots, and become healthy plants. Ultimately, what is planted there reaps a harvest of thirty, sixty, or even a hundred times the original amount of seeds dispersed. When I first heard the parable of the four soils, I thought, "That's what I want: the life with good soil that yields a good harvest." I've found that getting to that condition is a continual spiritual gardening project. With this short story, Jesus describes what holds us back from true spiritual growth. Learning about the four kinds of soil of the heart introduces us to new insights on unseen places that are vital to a healthy life where God's message and love grow in us.

Our wild lands within have various kinds of soil combinations, and sometimes these soils transform over time. Consider your own life. Have there been occasions when some of the "soil" of your heart was impenetrable? Things were so busy or hectic that nothing grew. Then at some point, that same path was harrowed into better soil, and God's word seemed to really take hold. Seeds in the soil of your heart germinated and plants started to grow. After a time, maybe that same soil was neglected and weeds showed up and choked out the plants. And perhaps in some seasons, the seeds landed on receptive soil of your heart. In those seasons, you may have seen remarkable growth and a wonderful harvest in store.

We can broaden the illustration even further. Rather than visualizing soil, seeds, and young plants, let's now imagine that what is unseen within us is an entire *world*, complete with a vast array of terrains, climates, weather conditions, and even some wild animals. This place needs navigation. Let's traverse and cultivate this interior place and ready it for the Divine Sower. God delights in lovingly renovating any wasteland within us into spectacular gardens, forests, and orchards and stunning vistas of all sorts. With attentiveness, our inner worlds can become beautiful and bountiful—not necessarily tame or domesticated but abundantly fruitful and wildly alive.

We can start by being curious. Using our curiosity, we can investigate some unknown and even uncomfortable places by first slowing down, settling close to the ground, and noticing. That's an approach we will use throughout this book: investigative curiosity. We will do this not only by learning with openness but also by engaging in spiritual practices with a receptive spirit to God's work. In the course of our lives, as God's work within us is nurtured through our cooperation and Scripture, mentors or spiritual companions, and other helpful tools like books, prayer practices, devotional activities, and learning opportunities, the land of our hearts becomes more fertile and will yield a more plentiful harvest.

The harvest will look like the fruit of the Spirit in our lives. In Galatians 5, the apostle Paul lists the fruit of the Spirit as love, joy, peace, patience, kindness, goodness, faithfulness, gentleness, and self-control. These are the very qualities of the Divine and of the Incarnation, Jesus the Christ. When we are planted and grown in the Spirit, we have the nature of the

Spirit. God brings about these qualities as we yield to the work of the Spirit in the wild land within.

Is It Worth It?

As we prepare to explore our inner terrains, you may be thinking, Is it worth it to take on such a challenge? Why do it? What will come from it?

If we turn down this holy calling to explore the wild land within—when we ignore the adventure and risk and persistent longing to enter this wild space—we leave a prize unclaimed. Until you are at ease and comfortable in your body, in the embrace of God, and with others, which occurs by doing this important inner work, you forfeit the salvation available freely to you now—not the salvation that the work of the cross has wrought but salvation from the intensity of unwholeness, feeling undone, and being ill at ease. I'm not saying everyone feels this way—a few dozen people are naturally cheery and chilled out and don't need much help at all. But for those of us who encounter darkness, dangers, and problems, there is a way forward. For those of us who have been told that Jesus is like a pill to fix our unease and ennui—then are left to wonder why this prescription doesn't seem to be working—there is a different way to get through the hardships. It makes sense that you've been confused, because you haven't received a fuller perspective.

Feeling the fullness of God's love and presence can happen only when we eventually attend to our wounds, insecurities, or self-loathing. By first exposing those places to ourselves and then handing them over to the love of our Maker, we then begin to become integrated into the ways and life of the spirit. The fancy word is *sanctification*. Some might call it a life of discipleship, which is an apt word to describe apprenticing ourselves to Jesus. But it's an ordinary progression in wisdom, growth, and understanding that vivifies our lives. Everyone who has seen difficult times and survived them and been transformed for the better can also attest to this.

God will always call us toward deeper, fuller lives. God beckons us toward more abundant joy and greater relief and solace. I take comfort for my own difficult journey in the sumptuous words of poet and *anam cara* John O'Donohue: "When you open your heart to discovery, you will be called to step outside the comfort barriers within which you have fortified your life. You will be called to risk old views and thoughts and to step off the circle of routine and image. This will often bring turbulence. The pendulum will fix at times on one extreme, and you will be out of balance. But your soul loves the danger of growth. In its own wise trust, your soul will always return you to a place of real and vital equilibrium."[1]

Healing and spiritual growth, after it happens, look and feel like peace, gracious integration of yourself, and (felt) access to love and grace. Before then, substantial healing and growth may feel unsettling and scary. But you will eventually find yourself with less anxiety and more confidence coming from the Source within and outside yourself in fuller ways.

You stand here at the threshold, on the verge of the wild land within. Whether you take this journey now or put it off until a later time, God won't leave you to your own peril. God will still sing to you and call you by name into greater being and fullness of life. It will feel like longing. Your soul longs for belonging and wholeness, which is the wordless calling of Divine Love.

In the next chapter, we'll learn about some theological influences of Western and Eastern varieties of Christianity that created features in our inner landscapes. For Christians, and anyone who's ever been affected by Christians, these occurrences have shaped our interior climate. We will learn about certain men and women in the early centuries of the church who devoted their lives to spiritual transformation in the imitation of Christ. Also upcoming are prevalent concepts about sin, reconciliation, and God that create specific inner topography we know too little about. We will explore various notions about the inner life, terms for this territory over the ages, and how to restore these disintegrated pieces to wholeness for spiritual healing and transformation.

Spiritual Practice: Quaker Queries

The Society of Friends, also known as Quakers, use a series of ongoing questions to guide inward reflection and to nurture spiritual maturity. As a religious group, they do not ascribe to creeds, but they keep particular virtues and principles at the center of their lives and fellowship together. The typical queries provide a "gut check." This is a spiritual exercise for individual or collective use.

As a way to begin this book, and in the spirit of contemplative spiritual practice, I invite you now to ask the following adapted queries of yourself. Reflect on them with sincerity, and

2

MAPS OF OLD

Learning from Ancient
Christian Spiritualities

The desert is a proving ground. It lays us bare, and its austerity tests our resolve. Our inner worlds may contain desert places, places where we initially long for refreshment and company. Eventually, though, the quiet places of desert may bring us into a deeper knowing of ourselves, purifying us from that which thwarts and tempts.

In this chapter, we will look at some old maps of the interior desert: theologies and histories that influence western Europe and the Western Hemisphere of the world. Some old maps we'll discuss have held too much sway, and their dogmatic cartography has overshadowed their usefulness. We will also look at some of the Eastern Christian ideas that didn't expand too much into the West but offer us a lush and frequently overlooked oasis of spiritual nourishment. These Eastern, or

Orthodox, spiritual teachings are deeply Christian concepts, rooted in the earliest days of Christianity as a religious movement. I have found many of these ancient "maps"—ways of knowing—to be indispensable for navigating the wild land within. They help us find ways through the desert, toward healthy spiritual formation and growing the fruit of the Spirit.

Desert Teachings

In the third and fourth centuries CE, after hundreds of years of extreme persecution and slaughter by the Roman Empire, Western Christianity transmogrified into the endorsed religion of the Empire. It was then that positions of clerical authority and advantageous career opportunities arose in the urban centers. Christianity was now culturally mainstreamed and attached to status. The wealthy and well-connected found ways to advance in the ranks of the emerging religious regime that now had the backing of the Roman state.

Common folks and devoted followers of Jesus noticed a terrible and compromising shift: a way of faith and community had restyled into an implement wielded for political power. Originally, the people who followed the ways of Jesus knew him as a humble healer, teacher, and impoverished prophet who fed the poor, healed the sick, and was crucified by the Roman Empire for insurrection. But by this period, followers of Jesus had the Christian belief system. It was systematized, organized, and institutionalized. With new government support, it was now being co-opted for the aims of wealth, politics, and power in the worldwide empire of the Caesar, headquartered in Rome.

This shift resulted in a migration of followers of Jesus, by the thousands, to abandoned desert wild places. They left cities like Alexandria, Rome, and Antioch for the wasteland places of Egypt and Syria. These fervent desert elders—or fathers (*abbas*) and mothers (*ammas*), as they were called—were Christian people choosing a difficult way of life on purpose. It was a new kind of martyrdom.

The desolate climate was an important feature of their chosen locations. Before his three-year ministry, Jesus went into the barren wilderness and fasted for forty days, and then the devil tempted him, according to Matthew, Mark, and Luke. The desert was the proving ground for Jesus, and his devotees in the third and fourth centuries decided to follow his example in this way.

Out in the lonely desert places, a man who would come to be called the Father of All Monks, Anthony of Egypt (251–376 CE), was said to be routinely tempted, attacked, and tortured by demons. Anthony, a greatly admired and a sought-after spiritual teacher, has a saying attributed to him that speaks to both life in the desert and the prevalence of temptation for us all: "Whoever has not experienced temptation cannot enter into the kingdom of heaven. Without temptation no one can be saved."[1]

As desert dwellers, these spiritual people sought to be transformed by a simple life of inner devotion, prayer, work, isolation, meager living, and poverty. This lifestyle is called asceticism, and they were ascetics. The word *ascetic* comes from the Greek word *askesis*, meaning "exercise" or "training." The Greek word evokes notions of training similar to preparation for athletic events. The ascetics wanted to train themselves in the ways of Jesus and give up everything of "empire Christianity" and its luxuries so that they might not lose their own souls. Theologian and priest Richard Finn writes, "Asceticism is seen in the ancient theologies as a journey towards spiritual transformation, where the simple is sufficient, the bliss is within, and the frugal is plenty."[2] At the peak of the desert-spirituality era, the desert mothers and fathers numbered about a whopping half million!

Sometimes these ascetics lived in what were the precursors to monastic religious communities. Many lived alone as hermits in small, simple dwellings called cells. Eastern Christianity, what is now often called Orthodox Christianity, embraces this variety of spirituality as their religious heritage. Writer Vladimir Lossky explains, "Orthodox Christian theology is *apophatic* in nature; this means that although God is personally known and experienced through [God's] divine energies, [God's] 'essence' [and] incomprehensibility remains absolute."[3]

In learning the spirituality of the wilderness places from our desert elders, we find a vital starting point for our own journeys inward. More than anything else, ascetics spent their time in prayer. They prayed unceasingly for the church, but mainly, they allowed prayer to quiet their hearts and lives. Some abbas and ammas taught others in the ways of asceticism and spiritual fidelity. The few who were educated and skilled did translation work. To pay for basic living expenses, they often did some kind of manual labor for part of the day. Some made baskets, rope, or consumable items, like bread or cheese. Some communities gardened or did animal husbandry for eventual transactions in the marketplace. Many spiritual seekers regularly journeyed from the cities into the desert to seek these desert elders for their teaching, guidance, and prayers.

Some visitors would also take up the ascetic lifestyle for a time. Ascetic devotion was an endeavor to literally imitate how Jesus lived, with nothing to call his own: no power, money, possessions, or status. Renowned desert hermit Evagrius Ponticus—who we will get to know a bit more in chapter 5—wrote invaluable guidance for ascetics about withstanding the deprivation of the desert to purify themselves in complete devotion to God, by imitating Jesus, through the power of the Holy Spirit. While most of us will never live as desert ascetics, we will learn from the ways and wisdom of these desert elders as we navigate the interior deserts within ourselves.

West Meets East

By the early medieval period in Europe, the Eastern and Western traditions of Christianity had noticeably different spiritual expressions. In the fifth century, John Cassian of Rome, a Western Christian, went to study with Evagrius Ponticus in the desert of Lower Egypt. There he learned the wisdom and ways of the ascetic life and the robust spiritual life of the monastic communities of the Eastern Christians. He then brought back these insights, mixed with some of his own, to Rome and the Christianity of the West. These writings still profoundly influence Western monastic religious life today. His work *Conferences of John Cassian* is directly referenced by the man most influential to the dramatic rise and prominence of monasticism in the West for a thousand years, Benedict of Nursia (480–547 CE).

Over time, the spiritual vocabularies in Western and Eastern Christianity diverged from each other. Certain spiritual concepts became altered as they were lost in translation among divergent cultures. For instance, the word *contemplation* that we use in English comes from the word *contemplatio* in Latin. The Latin word was interpreted from the transliterated word *theoria* in Greek. The Greek word *theoria* is where we get our English word for "theater" and refers to how something is understood wisely or is intellectually illuminated—not by the reasoning part of the brain but with one's attention as an engaged spectator. The Latin word *contemplatio* is meditation as it relates to prayer: the inner disposition that is absent of image, concept, and language, in which one prays with the heart. The divergence may seem subtle enough, perhaps, but over time, the distinctions grew and ossified into differing spiritual understandings and even doctrine. In the West, the Latin understanding of the word *contemplation* stuck, and the original Greek spiritual understanding all but evaporated. It is helpful for us to learn and reconcile both Eastern and Western understandings as we grow in spiritual formation to see the abundance available to us.

Evagrius's theological and spiritual understanding was most shaped by thinkers in early Orthodox Christianity: Coptic Christians, Oriental Orthodox Christians, the spiritual teacher Origen, and others who were some of the earliest Christian theologians with Middle Eastern milieus rather than European, Hellenistic, or Roman ones. Evagrius taught Christian concepts with an Eastern sensibility as it first developed in and near Jerusalem. Jesus was Jewish and taught Jewish men and women.[4] Centered within Evagrius's teachings are ancient and decidedly Jewish, and therefore Eastern, ideas—ones with holistic perspectives compared to Western dualistic doctrines.

Empire Influence

One of the stealthiest power brokers still affecting the spiritual lives of Christians in North America—and other places of Western European and Western Christian influence—is the Roman Empire. Even though the Roman Empire fell in the fifth century CE, it still holds sway in our spiritual understandings, and it still shapes our spiritual formation in countless ways to this very day. Most of these presumptions are not as present in the earliest forms of Eastern and Orthodox versions of Christianity where spiritual understandings were not minted in political power structures but are rooted deeply in the life of Jesus and spiritual teachings of the desert mothers and fathers. In fact, the original Eastern Jewish teachings of Jesus and of early Christianity became so overpowered by the Hellenistic worldview of the Roman world that it's a tricky task to disentangle it all now. Certain foundational concepts that we in the West understand as common to Christianity would actually seem like heathen ones to Jesus and Jesus's apostles.

A few centuries after Jesus and his first students walked the earth, the Empire was centralized in the Western Christian paradigm where it hadn't been centered previously. Eventually, for reasons I won't get into in this book, a schism broke fellowship between the Eastern Orthodox Church and the Catholic Church in Rome in 1054 CE. The rupture between the Greek East and the Latin West was made official and permanent. Despite the formal split, however, we who are Catholic or Protestant in the West can find tremendous wisdom from our spiritual forbearers in the wilderness places and from our Christian siblings in the East.

For the rest of the chapter, we'll look at the ways that empire thinking shaped Western Christianity and thus the fixtures in our inner worlds. We will also learn of the rich possibilities available as we turn toward the Eastern stream of Christian spirituality as a resource.

Much of the legacy of Western Christianity is bequeathed in forms of dualism: a view of the world that assumes unhelpful or patently false dichotomies. This array of distinctions and separations—among head and heart, soul and body, human and the natural world, material and spiritual—create distortions in our interior climates. Such a lens warps our perspectives about reality and can stunt spiritual growth.

For example, a common conception in the West is that the body is carnal, sinful, and corrupt and that it inexorably leads humans into moral failures. Christianity in the East retained a more Jewish sensibility about creation and the material world. God made our bodies and created the material world, Eastern Christianity maintains, and what God has made is good. We read this in Genesis. This central idea—of the essential goodness of God's creation—saturates Jewish and early Christian understanding. From it come specific ideas about how we operate in the world and even how we can feel valuable instead of perpetually ashamed. Our failures to understand and inhabit our embodiment have led us to true spiritual disintegration. Racism, colorism, sexism, xenophobia, and all manner of "othering" begin to occur when bodies are detached from the whole human organism as blessed creations. What we are left with are ways to objectify, vilify, commodify, and fear our own bodies and other bodies because we have not loved, made peace with, or felt at home in our own.

Eastern Christian thinking understands the power in the paradigm of wholeness. Paramount is the idea that Jesus is God made flesh. We too, as humans, have the hope of being perfectly united to God as Jesus was, perhaps within this lifetime on earth. By the power of grace, union with God is not considered a heretical idea but a holy aim. The body is not disgusting or inherently corrupt; it is a holy and beautiful temple of the Divine. In the West, we tend to believe or act as though our corrupt and defiled material nature cannot merge with Holy God, who is Spirit.

Upon closer consideration, we may notice that Western religious conceptions of spiritual formation can tend toward the more cerebral and academic, while Eastern concepts can tend to be more incarnational and embodied. Let's look further at some of the ways that other maps of Western dualism have misinformed many of us about the spiritual life, and let's get acquainted with some life-giving but lesser-known paths that Eastern Christianity offers.

Crime and Punishment

One way we see the lasting power of the Roman Empire in our wild lands within is by noticing how the fulcrum of our spiritual understanding is squarely based on the legal system. Empire conceptions of sin and redemption focus on something indispensable to a dominant military superpower: a society fixated on crime and punishment. Because of the Roman Empire, crime and punishment became the framework that served to fix the "problem of evil" in the West.

Feel the weight of that last statement. It is worth reading a few times.

It's true: the Roman penal system has likely affected the way you understand God, the way you view your actions, and even how you sense the presence of Divine Love in your everyday life. We cannot underestimate how influential the paradigm of crime and punishment is in the spiritual formation of most Western Christians. This knowledge gives us an excellent vantage point to view great swaths of the terrain of our lands within.

For most Western Christians today, this focus on crime and punishment is central to repentance and faith. For many of us, this reaches so deeply and thoroughly into our interior worlds that we can hardly comprehend all its effects. We still say that sin is "committed," like we say a crime is "committed"—though there are many ways one can perceive what is actually happening when sin happens. A focus on transgression language is a decidedly Western-cultural flavoring.

The crime and punishment paradigm holds sway over both Roman Catholic and Protestant thought in the West. For some of the Protestant reformer leaders in the sixteenth century, original sin was believed to have destroyed the human's freedom, or free will, to do good. A human can only sin.[5] This notion has an immense consequence in terms of one's ideas about spiritual formation.

For Roman Catholics, the sacrament of baptism expunges original sin.[6] After that, the regular *confession* of sin is required. Formal confessions said to a priest—who serves as a conciliator—are usually met with questions about the particulars of the sin. Which sorts of sin? In what circumstances? How many times? Then the violations are given verdicts by this mediator figure. This verdict includes penances that fit the crimes. In this way, the entire situation of being human, and the inevitable failures that come with it, is regularly treated as a kind of tribunal.[7] In Protestantism, less attention is paid to the personal or communal confessions that the Scriptures direct us to do regularly. Sin—viewed as crimes or offenses that we do or that are done to us—creates scars in the inner terrain.

In Western Christianity, our reconciliation to God is viewed like this: The human owes a moral debt, which is paid by Jesus of Nazareth being sacrificed through capital punishment on a Roman cross. God is the Judge who accepts this payment and declares humans "not guilty." This is not the view in Christianity of the East, as we will soon learn.

Western Christianity is beholden to empire notions of crime and punishment in other domains as well, including the atonement, or why Jesus died on the cross. There are a number of ways to understand what happened on the cross based not on the legal system of the Roman Empire but on Jewish and early Christian theology, history, and context.

Other formidable influences of the Roman Empire include Western images of God as a Zeus figure, the focus on divine retribution and punishment in hell or purgatory, and the dogma of God's wrathful judgment, which sometimes includes the dispensation of a violent apocalypse at the end times. Christianity in the East is far more comfortable with God as Divine Mystery and with the family relationship as a picture of Divine Love (the Trinity). Spiritual practices from the desert elders can reacquaint us with the Divine through a nonempire lens.

Restoration and Wholeness

For the early church in the first century, the very real problem of sin was approached differently, and the legal system was not the default paradigm for understanding sin or overcoming it. The word for "repentance" in ancient Greek is transliterated to *metanoia*, and it means "changing one's mind." This relates neither to a moral debt nor paying for a crime. For those in the East, repentance from sin doesn't relate to remorse, justification, or punishment; instead, it has to do with literally "turning around" toward something else. It involves a continual enactment of one's freedom, and this leads to restoration. This also means a return to the state before sin.[8]

Such an insight might completely upend how we view spiritual formation and transformation. It did for me. In the early years of my spiritual journey, I routinely felt that my relationship with God was defined by my rebellion. I thought of myself as an outlaw, frequently apprehended and on trial. I feared God's anger and punishment. This fear-based kind of living does not produce an ongoing harvest of abundant life of the Spirit, and it distracted me from growth toward Christlikeness. As I began to understand that a continual metanoia—returning to the embrace of God—is the spiritual journey itself and not something to be worried about and ashamed of, I found new delight in my life with God. I learned that the shepherd's rod and staff I read of in multiple Scripture passages, which had once registered to me as God's punishment and anger, instead guide us gently to life-giving safety, water, and pasture.

In the East, the act of Christ on the cross is not a legal transaction but an act of reconciliation. We are involved in ongoing *theosis*, which means transformation into the likeness of God and eventual union with God. Eastern theologies conceive that God initiates the redemption process but that humans, in our actions and attitudes, accept the perpetual ministry of the Divine.[9] This perspective further invigorates our ideas of the spiritual formation and growth process.

In the East, the inherent goodness of all God created and the human dependence on God are at the core of theological understanding. It is the starting point for understanding ourselves. We begin in wholeness, not deficit. With this understanding and a kind of medicinal insight, Evagrius offered diagnostic tools and guidance so students of Jesus could find total wellness through repentance and prevent sinning by living with a devout heart. Human fallibility and vulnerability, not ancestral moral debts, are at the center of the problem of sin, he said. In this understanding, the emphasis is on healing the sick rather than punishing the wayward. God's role as Savior is not through acting as a presiding Judge. God cares for us as the Great Physician and makes us well.

Confession in the East is handled in terms of broader spiritual development, and repentance is not confined to one's admission of misdeeds. Instead of going at it alone or finding a priest to mediate our absolutions, one chooses an elder as a spiritual guide to confide in. Spiritual directors and companions can offer a wide array of wisdom relating to navigating one's life and developing spiritual maturity over many years. One stays in a right relationship with God through a life carefully attended to God and turns back to God as soon as it is needed. Evagrius himself and many desert elders were selected as spiritual guides by a number of spiritually devout.

Disembodied Heads

Another legacy of the Roman Empire that commonly hampers our spiritual growth is the working notion that the brain is somehow separate from the body. This is simply not true, biologically or spiritually. The brain and the body function as a fully integrated unit. The concept that the brain is the seat of the intellect and the body is the vessel of instinct is a remnant of Western dualistic thought. It's a map we need to replace.

To create separate sectors for the mind and heart, or for the brain and body, is to create false dichotomies that impede our spiritual formation. These divisions often reflect far more about our cultural stereotypes, preferences, and prejudices than they do about any biological human reality or even our spiritual needs. This is very important to realize in terms of healing and growth. Not just personal restoration but also societal healing depends on an accurate understanding of wholeness.

The brain is the body. When our brains suffer, our bodies suffer, and vice versa, because no separation exists. If you have been traumatized as a child or victimized as an adult—say in a car accident or attack—the trauma has happened to the entire living organism of you, not just your rational brain and the language systems that might get engaged in talk therapy sessions. All of you must be engaged and involved in recovery and reintegration. Psychiatrist Bessel A. van der Kolk, MD, writes in *The Body Keeps the Score*, "Trauma victims cannot recover until they become familiar with and befriend the sensations in their bodies. Being frightened means that you live in a body that is always on guard. Angry people live in angry bodies."[10]

From a point of dualism, becoming dissociative and inflicting malice onto "othered bodies" is far easier than finding healing through wholeness.

In Western contexts, the notion of feeling connected to the full substance of ourselves is largely unfamiliar. This is even true in contexts of professional therapy or counseling, Christian or otherwise. Resolving shame, sinfulness, trauma, and conflict must happen with maps that see us as total organisms, not separated and disparate pieces. The biological reality that we are indeed connected and whole as *beings* gives us the best template for both healing and spiritual growth.

We commonly consider the heart as the seat of emotions within a person, with the beating organ in the chest metaphorically synonymous with passion and feelings. Usually, it is considered the not-too-rational or reasonable part of us. Many suppose that the heart is linked with romantic love, compassion, or perhaps the starting point for such things like our drives, motivations, and ambitions. Phrases like "He has a lot of heart!" or "My heart went out to her" seem to imply this notion. I want to be clear that this is *not* the meaning of *heart* in this book.

In fact, using only the word *heart* is something I will try to avoid within the following pages in favor of other words and phrases that can be more descriptive. You've already read other terms, like *land within, inner life,* and *interior world.* These are all ways to make the word *heart,* which has become trite or ambiguous, a bit less so.

Most of us don't think of our hearts as the place where thought comes from, metaphorically or otherwise; we consider that to be the job of the brain. From now on, let's consider "the land within" to consist of everything we think, feel, and sense and how we interconnect: the total unseen realm of us *and* between us. We don't usually realize that we function in such an incorporated, integrated, and interdependent manner. Instead, we've learned to split up all kinds of places within us, and it shows. Sometimes we live like our bodies are just the servants of our brains. We will now relearn and see anew.

Modern science confirms what early Eastern approaches to Christianity discovered and lived out: humans are *beings* who are integrated wholes, and we cannot separate our beings into distinct units of body, soul, heart, mind, emotions, and so forth. Dualism within humans is a lie.

We have consulted some ancient maps of the land within and found some to be more helpful than others. Presently, we are ready to do our own personal inner investigations and gardening work. I'm more hopeful that we may venture here without many of the contemporary presumptions of individualism and the same hindrances of empire that can so quickly undermine the work of spiritual formation.

It's a good time to ask, Where have I misunderstood my heart and mind as separate? In what ways has the false dichotomy of body and mind limited my understanding of myself or others? Have I been segmenting my inner world and not thinking of myself as a whole soul? What are the hidden influences of Western Empire Christianity on my views of life with God, sin, restoration, and growing in the Spirit?

In the next chapter, we'll hear from some voices we should have been learning from all along. They will not only ground us in the foundational ideas that Jesus revealed through his life and ministry; they will equip us for the most desperate perils of the land within and will ready us for deep growth and healing.

Spiritual Practice: The Examen

The Examen is a prayer form and a practice that began with Father Ignatius of Loyola (1491–1556 CE). Originally, it was used within the Ignatian spiritual exercises undertaken for discernment, spiritual maturity, and Christlikeness for those in and entering vocational priesthood. Since then, and now, all sorts of people find benefits in both the Spiritual Exercises and the prayer of Examen.

Ignatius recommended that the Examen be prayed at noon and at the end of the day. Most often people do the Examen before bedtime. When I do the Examen, I try to *start* my day with an intention of keeping God in mind throughout my day so that by bedtime, I have some memory of what happened. Otherwise, I can thoughtlessly move through my day, and then my time of Examen can feel puny and ineffective. Hopefully your memory works better than mine!

How to proceed during a time of Examen Prayer:

1. Come into quiet, and become aware of God's presence for a few moments. Then offer a prayer of thanksgiving. Start a mental review of your day (without judgment; just stick to the facts). Spend time reflecting on the events, the interactions, and your emotions throughout the day.

2. Also ask yourself these questions during the review: Where do I recognize God's presence today? Where was God's Spirit with me or someone else? In my thoughts and actions, when was I the most Christlike? When did I fall short?

3. Pay attention to your emotions, and ask God to be with you and give you grace, to heal you and make you more like Christ.

4. Ask for insight into the ways your responses were good, life-giving, or healing. Also ask God how you may have been insensitive, unloving, or damaging to others, creation, or yourself throughout your day. Then choose one feature of the day and bring it before God in prayer.

Each morning we are given new mercies. Offer yourself to God for the next day. Ask that you may be aware of God in your thoughts, actions, and relationships as you grow more fully alive to the presence of Christ with you in each moment.

CLIMATE AS CONTEXT

Centering Marginalized Voices

Our inner landscapes exist within climates that affect our spiritual formation. On earth, *climate* refers to a thirty-year average of weather and long-term patterns that interrelate within a climate system. For earth, the climate system includes the air, the water, the ice and permafrost, the upper rocky layer of the earth's crust, and all the living things within the area. On our planet, there are numerous climate zones: distinctive blends of temperature, terrain, vegetation, and air pressure that shape the lives of the inhabitants.

This is a solid corollary for the inner life. We can understand climate as both the seen and unseen components that shape the wild land within. A particular climate zone is created by one's childhood upbringing, economic class, education, family relationships, gender, sexual attractions, economic status, ethnicity, and race. In the previous chapter, we learned how Eastern and Western ideas could influence interior climates.

Other factors include our regional and personal religious, political, and spiritual influences and many more aspects in our society and culture. Even our digital and media connections affect our interior climates in countless ways. These climate factors alter how we relate to ourselves and others each day and how we form or malform, spiritually speaking. They modify how we perceive the agency and action of God.

Ethnicity, race, gender, biology, economic status: These and other aspects of our identities play parts in our spiritual growth too. All these aspects interrelate within our inner climate zones. Yet climate is often invisible to us and goes undetected, under our radars. Climate is familiar, unquestioned, and opaque. We also tend to project our own climate zones onto others without realizing how distinctive someone else's inner experience must be. In fact, one or two zones can become so pervasive that other kinds are imperceptible.

We need to regularly ask ourselves, What have I been perceiving as a "normal" climate? Does this particular theology or spirituality apply to everyone? Is a certain group being centered here in how I perceive this? Is a group with a certain background or history being excluded? All hidden influences allow us to misperceive reality. Too often we make uninformed decisions or harbor unchecked attitudes based on faulty presumptions. These climate misperceptions put our spiritual growth askew or in danger of malformation. We can learn to name the factors that alter—and sometimes pollute—our spiritual formation and personal growth.

Personal Influences

Consider for a moment what or who has most powerfully influenced your personal spirituality. Your greatest spiritual influence might have been a mother who wouldn't allow any talk of spirituality or religion in the home. Or maybe your parents were evangelical missionaries in China for decades. Either way, the people who raised you influenced how you experience who you think of as God. What are some of your main influences?

My parents met while singing in a seminary choir. They both came from a branch of institutional Christianity that was extremely conservative, Protestant, and Western: influenced by the Enlightenment and centered on a Western European understandings of the gospel. My Puerto Rican father was educated to be a minister within a Euro-colonized context. It didn't have much room for cultural flexibility or doctrinal nuance. Unfortunately, this sect of Christianity also identified most of his Latin American culture, including norms, customs, and music as sinful or inappropriate. You might say the rule of thumb was, "If it didn't seem white, it just wasn't right." Converts had to conform to extremely specific ways of looking, speaking, and behaving. There was no dancing (any rhythmic body movement), no movies, no alcohol, no wearing pants at church if you were a woman, no playing cards, and a huge list of banned music and books.

Like plenty of people of many backgrounds, my father didn't understand that this framework was rooted not in the claims of the gospel but rather in the claims of white cultural supremacy. He embraced these presuppositions and became indoctrinated by these views. Claims of white supremacy rarely look like actual burning crosses or lynching trees. They come baked in. They might show up as offhanded remarks, stereotyping others, rude jokes, assumptions, and everyday "othering" that reminds everyone of how society is supposed to work. These are sometimes called microaggressions. As a minister, my father would aim to convert others to the same flavor of Christianity to which he had been converted, as he conceded to the supposition that Euro-white culture was the superior one. Ultimately, this cultural erasure levied a hefty cost for him and for my family, as it did for countless others. As a result, I now write with an awareness of white-centeredness and colonization. As you might guess from what we learned in the previous chapter, this theological tradition in which my parents were schooled was steeped in Western dualism. It splits people within, and the contradictions lead to pain, isolation, and sorrow.

As you move through this chapter, think about your childhood and your past, and note what has influenced you or what has affected your life. As you developed, what ways of understanding God needed to mature? What ways of understanding yourself needed to be rectified? What needs to shift now?

The often-overlooked history and spiritual contexts of Native American, Latinx, Asian, and Black Christians help us understand and deepen our spiritual formation when we make the time to learn. In my context—the United States—the spiritualities of these minoritized groups are inextricably bound in the history of suffering and the brutalities from the conquest of the Americas by Europeans. Given the horrors that many people of color have endured, spiritual insights from these traditions can breathe wisdom, life, and hope into the most desperate of life's situations. By their resilience, continued survival, and instances of thriving, Black, Indigenous, Latinx, and people of color (BILPOC) are a testament to the most potent parts of what it means to be human. BILPOC spiritualities embody ways to be sustained by the Divine and enlighten us about the power of community. These can also dethrone our faulty presumptions about individualism as it relates to spiritual growth.

The plurality of voices and the varied histories create distinctive features within our inner landscapes that may lead to future fertile lands, once understood. To be American or to live in America means to encounter these realities firsthand. Outside of the United States, the pluralities may differ but the primary concept remains. For leaders or churches to see themselves as authorities in spiritual formation *without* a full examination of the dominant church's complicity in supremacy claims or violence is harmful. Indeed, for our spiritual formation to be healthy and Christlike, we must authentically reckon with our history in full.

Native American Spiritualities

The people groups, languages, religious beliefs, mythologies, and cultures of the Native people of North America are exceedingly varied. Information about these histories and spiritualities would require multiple volumes. As we take a brief glimpse at some American Indigenous understandings of spirituality, my hope is to both refute some misconceptions and spark your interest in seeking a greater understanding of this rich source of wisdom. We have so much to learn. We have so many wrongs to put right.

In the sixteenth century, powerful European interests were determined to colonize and convert Native populations of the Americas to some variety of Christianity. The Indigenous people of North America alone numbered more than fifty million. In contrast to the countries backed by the pope in Rome, the settlers of British colonies in New England were usually Protestants. These Protestant traditions had rejected and opposed Roman Catholicism. One of the few exceptions was the British settlements of Catholic refuge called the Chesapeake Colonies, founded originally in 1606—which later became the state of Maryland and some parts of the state of Virginia.

British religious efforts in the New World did not have the same systematic or funded enterprises to evangelize and convert the Native residents of the Americas as did the Portuguese or Spanish crowns. Protestants had been inculcated to value and expect comprehensive changes in custom, behavior, and lifestyle following a conversion to Christianity. This meant converts to Christianity had to assimilate to all the European cultural norms and customs. Exhibiting these changes to European Christian values and customs was compulsory for new converts. Roman Catholics sometimes forced conversions but were usually more flexible in expressions of Christian practice. In regions of North America, Central America, and where the Spanish ruled, elements of local customs, rituals, festivals, holidays, and ceremonies were tolerated. Some were included somehow in Catholic observances and added to Catholic expressions of religious life and devotion.

For the Protestant Puritan settlers from England, in particular, any combination of Native American culture or practices with Anglo-Protestant Christian doctrines and activities was intolerable and prohibited. European Protestant settlers often viewed the Indigenous residents in the Americans as vulgar obstacles that needed to be expelled from areas that settlers wanted.

Starting with the laws and actions of the colonizing British government and following a series of decisions of the US Supreme Court that culminated in 1823, the public international law called the Doctrine of Discovery was used to lay claim and take land from Indigenous people in any non-Christian so-called discovered land.[1] Eradicating Native Americans and their ways was often high on the to-do list as Europeans continued their move westward and encroached onto more Native American lands and people groups. There were attacks, on combatant and peaceful tribes alike, where children, women, and men were attacked and slaughtered.

In the landmark decision of *Johnson v. M'Intosh*, Chief Justice John Marshall explained that tribes had only a right of occupancy. They had neither property rights nor complete sovereignty at the moment the land was found by a discovering Christian European nation. Thus the US government made it legal to purchase or take by conquest all the land in America from its Native residents.[2] This law also privileged the Christian religion, as it also normalized and legitimized continual warfare campaigns against the Native population, justified their relocation to inhospitable areas, and condoned their eradication. Such violence was also validated by portions of the Old Testament—for example, when Israelite leader Joshua killed off the inhabitants of the Promised Land of Canaan. The white people of European descent took dominion over the Americans and eradicated its inhabitants because they believed that they were truly God's chosen people in the Promised Land that was rightfully theirs.

Systematically, Native Americans were forced onto specific acreage allotments on barren sites often very far from their homelands. Neither voting rights nor freedom of religion or worship was afforded to them. After that, the US government separated Native American children from their parents. These children were taken from their homes and communities and confined in government boarding schools usually run by Protestant Christian missionaries. Native Americans were forced to cut their hair into European styles and made to wear European-style clothing. The children were forbidden to speak their own languages or practice any of their tribal or spiritual rituals or customs. This swift assimilation was also closely associated with the aims of national patriotism and backed by assumptions of white supremacy. The last of these schools ran until the 1970s.

Dr. George Tinker, a member of the Osage Nation, has examined Native American theology and liberation in the context of white Christian settlers. Dr. Tinker explains that from the onset, European colonizers believed their ways of life and religious beliefs were superior, and their behavior underscored their disdain. White settlers considered Native Americans to be "'uncivilized' barbarians," according to Tinker: "They were cast as 'unfriendlies' or 'hostiles' who [would] 'raid' Christian settlements across the continent." Native Americans, writes Tinker, "live in constant awareness of the history of consistent and persistent euro-christian violence associated with the conquest of Native lands and peoples, a history that is largely forgotten among our euro-christian relatives, hidden away in the unconscious fog of denial and myth-making."[3]

For eighty years, the Iliff School of Theology, where Tinker taught in Colorado, publicly displayed a book that was given as a gift to the institution. The book was called *The History of Christianity*, and it was bound and covered in the skin of a Native American man who had been killed by a settler in western Virginia. After his death, the man's skin was flayed from his body and tanned to be used as human leather. It became the human-leather cover for the book. The theology school not only received the gift as though it was an honor; it showcased the book with pride from 1893 until sometime in 1974.[4] This desecration of human remains was, of course, a gruesome offense to the Native Americans. The book was a macabre trophy of conquest that exhibits the depravity of the owner who presented it as a gift to the school and the school's inability to see Native Americans as equal in their humanity and worthy of parallel respect.

Native Americans are routinely misrepresented, misunderstood, and overlooked. Their cultures are often minimized, mischaracterized, and viewed through a prejudiced and puerile Western European lens. Added to this are the stereotypes, exploitations, and rampant misinformation in movies, media, literature, sports mascots, and other forms of communication that depict Native Americans unfavorably. The profound and long-standing enmity and repugnance many whites feel toward Native American people are not things of the past. Native Americans still suffer persecution, violence, and death at the hands of white people at rates higher than any group in America per capita.[5]

A common misconception regarding the theology and spirituality of Native Americans is that they worship nature. At minimum, this is a clumsy mischaracterization or even patently false. Generally speaking, among the North American Native people groups, there is a recognition that God (or Great Creator or Great Spirit) is *beyond* nature. Overall, this does not pose a direct conflict with basic Christian theology.

Most Native American clans adhere to a belief in a sacred connection to ancestors, who live in a "land of the dead" or in a parallel world in the sky, or less frequently, in a place of the dead underground or below the water. Cultural customs, ceremonies, and religious observances often intertwine and infuse the wisdom of the sacred spiritual realm. Most groups in their ceremonies involve the departed with those actively participating in the observance in some way. This understanding is not that far removed from how the New Testament author of Hebrews 12:1 describes those who have died and gone before us as the "great cloud of witnesses."

Native American ceremonies typically involve the community. People as a group interact with the divine or the spirit world through a spiritual mediator. Some myths (like those related to the Sun Dance and the Ghost Dance) are connected to traditional religious rituals involving movement and dance, drumming, vocalizing, trance, and song.

Because of long-standing and widespread mistreatment and genocide, many Native Americans harbor a deep disdain for Christianity, and some Christian Native Americans are considered traitors within the community.[6] Within contemporary expressions of Christian spirituality among Native Americans, some groups are reviving traditional practices within the framework of the gospel message and Christian expressions. This includes such things as burning tobacco, cedar, sweetgrass, and sage; cooking and serving traditional food, like buffalo and wild rice; and incorporating traditional dance and drumming during songs.

What emerges clearly is that the spiritualities and ways of the original residents of America are not segmented into parts like Western Europeans. Their lives are thoroughly spiritual. Unlike many in modern American culture, they are deeply grounded in a connection with the natural world, their families, and the animating life force that comes from the Source of all things. Native American poet Joy Harjo, a member of the Muscogee (Creek) Nation in Oklahoma and poet laureate of the United States, has called God the "Breath-Giver." This name for God can add to our sense of God's nature and the potent gift of life that begins simply with an inhalation of air into our lungs.

African Spiritualities in the Americas

To understand the spiritualities of the people of African diaspora in the United States, a basic understanding of the historical and ongoing subjugation and maltreatment is crucial. To people groups who have been silenced, the contemplative and spiritual practices that transform are ones of liberation and expression. Dr. Barbara A. Holmes notes in her illuminating book *Joy Unspeakable: Contemplative Practices of the Black Church* that deeply contemplative activities in the Black church emerge from a "besieged people." The language of prayer and the impetus for prophetic proclamation and action arise from one's sacred interior spaces.[7] Instead of being quiet and using silence to find stillness and peace for the soul, proclamation, movement, shouts, moans, call-and-response, clapping, dancing, singing, and action in the real world are some of the hallmarks of contemplative and spiritual practice in the American Black church.

Let us listen and learn from the spirituality of the Black church: what is drawn from the heart of God in the interior life punctures the faulty sacred-and-secular divide. We must center these voices within our understanding as we form spiritually.

Something drastic happened in the 1450s. Though people with darker skin pigmentation were "othered" by lighter-skinned Europeans for eons, Prince Henry of Portugal embarked on a grim enterprise with the full support of the church in Rome. As the Indigenous people in colonized South America quickly succumbed to European diseases or died from maltreatment and forced labor during the first years of conquest, Prince Henry devised a business plan to capture and traffic people from Africa as replacements. Most Africans were already resistant to the many European diseases that would eventually annihilate millions of Indigenous people in the colonized Americas. Prince Henry commissioned propaganda from writer Gomes Eanes de Zurara, and so began the official construct of race for commercial gain.

De Zurara used the physical features common in dark-skinned West Africans to leverage the fiction that Africans were a separate, more primitive subspecies of humans. *Negro* means the color "black" in Portuguese and Spanish. His writings convinced the general public and interested profiteers that Africans were biologically inferior to (light-skinned) Europeans.[8] The church then approved their vanquishing, enslavement, and even their conversion to Christianity by force. The authority of papal bulls from Pope Nicolas V in the 1450s gave approval and the accompanying financial backing and resources for these efforts. Thus European countries were authorized to enslave and traffic those from West and West-Central Africa not merely as a workforce but for chattel as though it was the will of God.[9] The wreckage and legacy of this era on so many people's internal landscapes are incalculable.

The international human trafficking from Africa to many places around the globe was concomitant with rampant sexual predation, violence, systemic and structural racist laws, and all manner of human rights crimes. Enslaved Africans arrived in Virginia in 1619, and later the people, industries, churches, institutions, and the government of the United States of America—in both the North and the South—directly participated in the slave trade or benefited from it. After 1660, the Christian communities of the Chesapeake Colonies (parts that are now Virginia) created and enforced some of the cruelest sorts of laws toward other humans ever devised. They legally defined slavery as lifelong bondage. This was a departure from categorizing servitude based on biblical examples of debt bondage (bond servants) or indentured servitude, where a person could eventually obtain their freedom through working as a servant. The laws to profit enslavers were antithetical to Jewish statues of Jubilee and to the mission Jesus proclaims from the prophet Isaiah 61:1 NLT: "The Spirit of the Sovereign Lord is upon me, for the Lord has anointed me to bring good news to the poor. He has sent me to comfort the brokenhearted and to proclaim that captives will be released and prisoners will be freed."

Slavery was also made a heritable condition; all the children of enslaved mothers were automatically enslaved at birth. A life of ongoing horrors was common for those enslaved. The law made systematic sexual exploitation, impregnation, and rape of enslaved women a common occurrence in antebellum life. By 1860, Black slaves in the United States numbered nearly four million.[10]

Christian instruction was used by enslavers to create and maintain obedience and a social order where white slaveholders were at the top, as ordained by God. Church sermons to the enslaved often focused on passages of Scripture like Ephesians 6:5 to engender compliance with their own mistreatment and enslavement as sanctioned and part of God's will: "Servants, be obedient to them that are your masters according to the flesh, with fear and trembling, in singleness of your heart, as unto Christ" (Ephesians 6:5 KJV).

The legacies of Black American Christians—art, music, song, dance, styles of worship and preaching, and theologies—are spiritual treasuries created by surviving and overcoming these real-life nightmares.

There is no justice for all people of the United States without a reckoning with this past. There can be no full reconciliation or restoration without honesty and transparency about the crimes and inhumanity propagated on those of the African diaspora. We have to disrupt and dismantle the laws and systems that perpetuate the legacies of inequality and inequity.

One of the many gifts of Black theology is a unique understanding of God's presence in the midst of suffering, resilience during times of trials, and hope of new life seized from the clutches of despair and death. In his book *Jesus and the Disinherited*, published in 1949, theologian and mystic Dr. Howard Thurman explains how the life and teachings of Jesus offer real hope for the poor, marginalized, and oppressed—all those whose backs are "against the wall." He saw the religion of Jesus from Scriptures and the religion the slaveholders called

Christianity to be two very different things. Martin Luther King Jr. reported that he always had a copy of *Jesus and the Disinherited* with him at every march for freedom during the civil rights movement.

The theology and spirituality of the Black church center on the sustaining hope and deliverance of God. Black American theologian Dr. James H. Cone summarizes the salvific aspect of Black theology this way: "The Gospel of Jesus is not a rational concept to be explained in a theory of salvation, but a story about God's presence in Jesus's solidarity with the oppressed, which led to his death on the cross. What is redemptive in the faith is that God snatches victory out of defeat, life out of death, and hope out of despair, as revealed in the biblical and black proclamation of Jesus's resurrection."[11] Cone writes that the Christian gospel in the Black community is not a mere strategy for enduring hard times or for waiting for paradise. Rather, the gospel is "an immanent reality—a powerful liberating presence among the poor right now in their midst."[12]

In addition, womanist theology, or Black feminist theology, offers manifold wisdom often overlooked by dominant-culture Christianity. "Womanism is committed to the wholeness and flourishing of the entire community," writes womanist theologian Dr. Wilda Gafney. "Most simply, womanism is black women's feminism. It distinguishes itself from the dominant-culture feminism, which is all too often distorted by racism and classism and marginalizes womanism, womanists, and women of color."[13] Like feminism, which confronts societal preferences and biases while working to rectify inequality, womanism includes not only these efforts but also the emphases of the Black liberation movement. Black liberation celebrates African culture and physical aesthetics and works to emancipate lives. Both religious and nonreligious settings and various fields of study are part of the Black liberation movement.[14]

Latinx Spiritualities

The people included in the category of Latinx represent a wide swath of groups with diverse ancestries that have experienced the suffering and injuries of colonization. The legacy of Spain's conquest in the Americas lives on in the Spanish language shared across diverse groups. Countries with these legacies are referred to as Latin America. Much of South America, Central America, Mexico, and certain islands of the Caribbean were once under Spain's dominion. The Spanish conquest also included places where the states of California, Texas, New Mexico, Florida, and Arizona are located today. Some countries, like Cuba, declared their independence from Spain, while others, like my island of Puerto Rico, were seized from Spain and colonized as an American territory and then denied the rights given to citizens of a state, such as a citizen's right to vote for the US president or vice president or have voting representatives in the US Congress.[15]

Currently, in the United States, approximately twenty-five million Latinx identify as Catholic, and another nine million identify as (Protestant) Pentecostal or Charismatic.[16] Latinx, who may tend to look nonwhite, are the fastest-growing "othered" group in the United States. From the beginning, xenophobia was etched into the structure of the United States, and various nonwhite groups throughout US history have been systematically restricted from entering the country and excluded from naturalization and equal rights compared to preferred immigrants from Western, Central Europe, and Scandinavia with historically large majorities of light-skinned populations.

Latinx people are no monolith, politically or culturally, and each country within Latin America has its own unique history and ongoing story. Many varieties of Indigenous populations exist within Latin American countries as well, and they usually undergo their own forms of oppression and persecution by governmental authorities and nationals alike. Colorism and racism take their own nefarious forms in Latin American countries as a legacy of European conquest. Those of European ancestry still have most of the controlling interest in terms of property, wealth, opportunity, educational advantage, political position, and power.

Generally speaking, Latinx culture is far more collectivist than mainstream Euro-centered North American culture. There is a rich tradition of devotional practice that includes prayer, spiritual, and contemplative practices found in the Catholic mystic tradition originating in Spain. Latinx values include family and local community (*personalismo* and *familismo*). Familismo pertains to the integral role that the family relationships have in the everyday lives of Latinxs. Personalismo refers to warmth and closeness in relationships. It is this context that further generates the internal conditions for intimate and direct relationships with God that many Latinx people experience in their faith, writes Ada Maria Isasi-Diaz, a Latina theologian.[17] Dr. Isasi-Diaz coined the term *mujerista theology*, which is now used broadly as a liberation theology that contains space for the lives of women with Hispanic and Latin American heritage.

The spirituality of Latinx women is often related to the way their lives are harmed by mainstream society. These lives encompass oppressive limits, such as ethnic prejudice, intersectionality, sexism, and economic inequalities. Rather than keeping these viewpoints on the sidelines in our society and in our interests, they must gain mainstream exposure and influence in understanding how we spiritually form and malform.

Asian Christian Spiritualities

There are many ethnic groups in the US context that I cannot examine within the constraints of this book. That said, I will add one more segment of people that includes a panethnic group making up about 6.5 percent of the US population.[18] Currently, in the United States, people whose ancestry comes from or near the Asian continent are usually considered nonwhite. On official US government forms, Asians are asked to identify themselves as a separate race of humans. This does not hold true categorically in most of the rest of the world's countries.

Entry into the United States by Asian people began in large numbers during the mid-1800s. At this time, immigrants came mainly from China to the West Coast to begin new lives. Many arrived to work in mines during the gold rush in the West and contributed greatly to the building of the transcontinental railroad coming from the Pacific side. Their spiritual experiences are varied and have parallel qualities with others of minoritized and mistreated groups. To explore a very helpful aspect of Asian Christian spirituality and formation, we will soon learn about Minjung theology that arose out of the Christian experiences and national history in South Korea.

Liberative Theologies

Liberation theologies aptly challenge the dominance of empire Christianity that many of us take for granted. While liberation theology is often associated with the Latin American context, there are liberation theologies that emerge from various marginalized groups. Though once considered an outlier or even a menace to mainstream Christianity, these ideas of God's love invite us to reclaim the revolutionary, peasant, rabbi Jesus who disrupted the privilege of the ruling classes and confronted the powerful to help the outcast poor and treat their enemies with love.

Peruvian theologian and Dominican priest Gustavo Gutiérrez, born in 1928, is regarded as one of the principal founders of liberation theology. Because Gutiérrez has directly encountered many poor who suffer daily, his theological work distills spirituality in action. His are not removed ideas or propositional points of theology common in the academy. His work also explores the nature of God in a context of deprivation, injustice, and oppression.

In his commentary on Job, Gutiérrez expounds on unjust suffering as it relates to the contemplative life. In the anguishes of lived-out realities, the lowly people can find God and can deeply rest in God, who cherishes them and meets them where they are. The beatitudes offer counterpoints to life as usual; they offer a kingdom-of-God life that sees and honors the poor and disenfranchised. This life is not available to the prosperous.

Gutiérrez also explains how we become formed as we speak of God during the agonies and difficulties of oppression. He developed the foundational insight of Latin American liberation theology, what has been called "God's preferential option for the poor." To understand the unique contributions of spiritual thought and ways of being from this context, we must unpack this foundational phrase. It captures a sense of the compassionate heart of God that Gutiérrez and other liberation theologians further elucidate in their work.

Gutiérrez notes that "the poor" refers to those who are impoverished *materially*. The plight of the poor results in premature and unjust death. To the powerful, the poor remain statistical and nameless. But the poor are significant to God, says Gutiérrez. They must be significant to all who serve Christ. For those of us in affluent countries and situations, this should give us pause. Do we give significance to the poor? Do we realize that their lives are forever entwined with ours because God loves them?

There are also those who are poor *spiritually*. These are people who are *aware* of their need for God and are actively seeking God. In Matthew 5:3 KJV, Jesus tells us of them, "Blessed are the poor in spirit, for theirs is the kingdom of God." In either case, materially or spiritually, those who are rich must give what they have. Gutiérrez confronts us with the reality of what the materially poor encounter so that their plight and hardships can be alleviated.

The word *preferential* refers to two dimensions: the universal and the particular. Universally, God's love extends to all. In particular, God has a special "soft spot," as it were, for those in need. Liberation theology claims that God demonstrates special dispensations of grace to the poor, the downtrodden, and those excluded from a life of material sufficiency. We can find this evidenced scripturally numerous times: in the care and oversight of the societally excluded and impoverished through welfare statutes in the Levitical laws, in the many stories featuring underdog heroes in the Old Testament, and in the Incarnation of Christ as the underprivileged Yeshua, the Jewish peasant from the backwaters of Nazareth.

In Spanish, the word for *option* connotes a meaning that is closer to the English word for *commitment*.[19] It involves aiding the poor and standing in ongoing solidarity with them. It also means standing *against* inhumane poverty. Most importantly, Gutiérrez underscores the idea of a commitment to the poor in terms of friendship so that objectification and abstraction do not begin to co-opt these efforts of solidarity. He says, "When we become friends with the poor, their presence leaves an indelible imprint on our lives and we are much more likely to remain committed [to help them]."[20]

Gutiérrez articulates how true "liberation" has three main dimensions in the internal and external worlds. First, it involves political and social liberation, the elimination of the immediate causes of poverty and injustice. Second, it involves the emancipation of the poor, the marginalized, the downtrodden, and the oppressed from all "those things that limit their capacity to develop themselves freely and in dignity." Third, it involves liberation from selfishness and sin and a reestablishment of a relationship with God and with other people.

Another unique contribution within the context of liberation theology comes from Asian spirituality in the form of an indigenous Korean theology. Minjung theology pulls from a word used during the Yi dynasty (1392–1910) to describe those outside the elite and ruling class—those people were called Minjung, meaning the crowd, or "masses of people." Minjung theology, which emerged in the 1970s, concentrates on the mission of Jesus to bring healing and freedom from oppression to those sinned against by *han*. *Han* is a Korean word meaning intense woundedness, sin sickness, or unresolved suffering. *Han* can also be "sown in the land." This was the case many times in Korean history during violent conquests and also in the United States with chattel slavery of those of African descent and genocide of the Native Americans. By remedying *han* and political and systematic injustice, the original vision of Jesus's kingdom can come to fruition.[21]

Gutiérrez and other liberation theologians show us that what is external radically affects our internal worlds and also that our internal fortitudes can and should bring change into the external world as we take action. Though the lives of BILPOC Christians often reflect hardship and marginalization, the vibrant spirituality and the gifts of scholars, teachers, and ordinary people of color cannot be underestimated or overlooked as we tend to our spiritual formation and allow God to re-create us.

We need the direct leadership and guidance of those who have been previously or are currently marginalized. Hosting panels and inviting representation is not enough. This is tokenization, and it does not dismantle oppressive systems. We must follow the lead of BILPOC people and other marginalized voices to make better worlds and opportunities for growth in our surroundings and within ourselves.

In the next chapter, we will go deeper into our lands within and explore the three most monumental features that plague our lives daily. There are specific spots in your inner world and mine that are damaged. For many of us, some places are fully shrouded in shadow, and yet their topography influences dozens of choices we make each day. These places also shape some of our most confounding troubles.

Spiritual Practice: Call and Response

Black people who were enslaved created and sang thousands of songs during and after the enslavement era. In the fields, homes, workplaces, and the hush harbors (clandestine church gatherings), these songs were some of the many unsilent, embodied, and communal contemplative practices. In Black churches across America, these songs remain mainstays, testifying to the strength of the human spirit and the mighty works of God. These lead to the gifts of communal response and perseverance, toward union with God.[22] We can seek a spiritual balance between individual piety and communal justice—seeking in the reflective activities of contemplation whether in prayer, song, or activities that foster social transformation and human flourishing.

The following chorus and verses are of a beloved Black spiritual based on Isaiah 60:1. I really enjoyed learning the melody to this song by doing an online search, and I think you would also. I invite you to sink deeply into the words and read them over a few times as well. Allow yourself to be moved by the experiences of trust in God that this song demonstrates. Read the song aloud. If you can, read this in a group context. Your group could do a call-and-response style, in which one person calls out the lyrics while everyone else sings the chorus and the repeating phrase "My Lord says He's coming by an' by."

RISE, SHINE, FOR THY LIGHT IS A-COMING

Chorus
O, rise! shine! for thy light is a-coming
Rise! Shine! For thy light is a-coming
O, rise! shine! for thy light is a-coming
My Lord says He's coming by an' by

I.
This is the year of Jubilee
My Lord says He's coming by an' by
My Lord has set His people free
My Lord says He's coming by an' by

Chorus

2.
I'm goin' to shout an' never stop
My Lord says He's coming by an' by
Until I reach the mountain top
My Lord says He's coming by an' by

Chorus

3.
O wet and dry I'm goin' to try
My Lord says He's coming by an' by
To serve the Lord until I die
My Lord says He's coming by an' by.

Chorus

CHASMS WITHIN

Naming Our Wounds

Sarah grew up in poverty. There was never quite enough to go around. She told me about the time her mother discovered an uneaten bakery cake still in its box in their neighbor's garbage bin. She made Sarah salvage it and bring it home. It was a delicacy they could never afford. But the shame of sneaking food from someone else's trash stung, and Sarah resolved to never be in poverty again. As a teen and adult, she strove to create financial security for her future as she fretfully saved every penny and worked nonstop. Sometimes, although she didn't like to admit it, she resented the lives of others who seemed to scamper up the ladder of success and find monetary security with ease. At her job, Sarah hustled and even steamrolled a few people to get ahead. Finally, she obtained the position in the high-paying career she wanted. The message throbbing in the background of Sarah's life was "Avoid the pain associated with feeling need."

This directed many of her decisions—sometimes consciously but usually just under the level of her awareness.

At about age five, Norman discovered that his parents liked it when he sang certain songs for his grandma. He loved to perform, but even if he was tired of performing, he would usually comply with the request in order to feel his parents' pleasure and to gain positive attention. Like all of us do in various ways, he learned that impressing people matters and the rewards are worth the effort. Sometimes the reward for unappreciated behavior feels worth it too. We may learn that sobbing when our parents ask us to keep singing gets Grandma to give us hugs and ice cream. As Norman matured, he became aware of his effect on others and grew emotionally dependent on how others perceived him. If friends accepted him, this created a pleasant measurement not only to understand his place in his world and determine his value to others but also to organize his own sense of himself. Over time, he felt increasingly awkward and uncomfortable if people seemed displeased or disappointed with him. It became harder for Norman to say no. He found himself agreeing to all sorts of things he didn't want to do in order to not upset others or give others a reason not to like him.

J was the oldest of seven siblings. Their parents were spread thin with the responsibilities of such a large family. They ran a strict home and demanded a lot from J, who bore the brunt of "parenting" several of the children. From the age of eight, J was expected to manage childcare. That meant cooking and cleaning, bathing and dressing, helping with homework, and all the rest. When they came up short—which felt often—J's father would fly into a rage. J noticed that children their age in other families often got to play outside all afternoon. Those kids could play games or read books, participate in sports, or visit friends, but J's homelife didn't afford them those same chances or much free time. Soon after J's eighteenth birthday, they escaped their home by joining the military and shipping out.

These three people are not so unlike ourselves and people we know. Their stories illustrate three aspects of our inner worlds that commonly become injured as we encounter life. We all operate out of wounds, many of which are at least partially invisible to us. Sarah, Norman, and J are aware of some of their wild lands within and are quite unaware of others. Because some of their own interior lives remain invisible to them, they make efforts or take on projects to remedy what feels like ongoing discomfort or outright pain.

Remember the quadrants of the Johari Window that we learned about in the first chapter? While we may be aware of certain parts of ourselves, we remain unable to see other influences. Becoming aware of aspects of our inner landscapes that are hidden can be difficult, but it's an essential task of cultivating wholeness. Let's begin to explore some of those areas more carefully.

Three Chasms

Imagine you are on top of a desert mesa and can gaze over all your inner world. Your view stretches for hundreds of miles. From this vantage point, you can see the rugged terrain below as well as steep and narrow trails leading toward large ravines that are hidden in shadows.

The interior world of each person has three ravines—core wounds—with which to contend. The gaps are unbridgeable. In reality, of course, none of us has a clear vantage point atop the mesa to see all three. In the language of the Johari Window model, a full view from the mesa would mean you are able to see all four quadrants. None of us can view ourselves entirely objectively and can perceive such things. The chasms form in our lives and remain within us. We reside in those dim and hidden areas and lose sight of the wider terrain.

We may stay put within these places without ever moving toward other terrains. We have little insight into our surroundings because the view is so obscured. We remain far too unknown to ourselves. Some of us have fumbled and felt our ways into the other ravines with great hardship, injury, and suffering.

Sometimes we migrate back and forth or take up very long residence in one particular shadowy and tangled chasm or another. No matter what, we never know too much about those darkened places until the Divine and healing light shines into each gulf, crevice, and cranny.

Wisdom of the ages has crafted winding paths that help us trek through these ravines and find our ways out again. But few of us find or follow those paths all the way out. If we find them and follow them at all, it often takes our whole lives to venture through them. Some of us have erected our own tent dwellings in one of the shadowed ravines, having decided it was safer to camp out there than to travel further on. Like Sarah, Norman, and J, I also know about these lowlands. I've lived in all of them—and with no hope of getting any mail or Wi-Fi. I didn't even know where I was.

In this chapter, we will look at the three perilous chasms of our inner lives that refer to the three core wounds that are part of our human experience. Father Thomas Keating speaks of these core wounds in his book *Invitation to Love: The Way of Christian Contemplation*. As humans, we all have three biological needs that are essential: safety and security, esteem and affection, and power and control. Our three core wounds correspond to these three vital needs. When our needs for safety and security, esteem and affection, and power and control go unmet, core wounds are formed like chasms within. Keating explains that we experience spiritual transformation when we heal the unconscious motives and responses that have become ingrained habits within us.

Chasms in our interior worlds, these core wounds, will detract from the relationship with the Divine. They can prevent us from knowing ourselves and being gracious to ourselves, such that growth becomes difficult or impossible. And core wounds can wreak havoc with our relationships with others. Furthermore, when we function from inside these chasm wounds, we hamstring so many of our efforts in vocation and life. When inadvertently taking up residence in a chasm of woundedness—whether it's a massive ravine or a small gully—we start to feel trapped. We may have no idea why, and we may go on for years floundering, wounded, and restless.

Be assured that we *all* have issues like this in our interior worlds. We all carry some core wound issues within us—needs and injuries that contribute to our sense of safety and security, esteem and affection, and power and control. I can tell you that change is possible and healing is findable—but not by chance.

Safety and Security

We come into the world as helpless infants with basic needs to be fed and kept safe. Usually a bond between mother and child also ensues. Relational bonding is vital for humans, as it is for many other social mammals, such as cats, dogs, elephants, monkeys, and thousands of other species. In many mammals, all other relational connections are afflicted if this early bond is significantly disrupted. Adequate amounts of safety and security in these early weeks, months, and years create healthy foundations for a human to continue to feel safe and secure as an adult.

Circumstances like poverty, prolonged illness, disaster, instability in the home, disability, parental sickness or death, homelessness, refugee status, and other issues can create lasting deficits when they occur during this early stage of life. "Traumatized people chronically feel unsafe inside their bodies," writes trauma expert Dr. Bessel A. van der Kolk. "The past is alive in the form of gnawing interior discomfort. Their bodies are constantly bombarded by visceral warning signs, and, in an attempt to control these processes, they often become expert at ignoring their gut feelings and in numbing awareness of what is played out inside. They learn to hide from their selves."[1] When things go wrong early on, lifelong damage can develop. Healing and recovery are necessary, or the trauma will influence other relationships and get passed along to offspring.

Most often these traumas, whether large or small, become flattened and generalized. With a few exceptions that we might remember as "flashbulb moments," we don't have the capacity to remember the actual situations that caused the most harm early on, says Keating. Traumas often happen outside of the organizing contexts of language or of conscious and chronological memory. Or even if we can remember and talk about early trauma, our interpretations of the events remain only partial understandings of reality. Each time we access a traumatic memory, our current emotions attach to and slightly alter the memory itself. Then we remember not really the event but the memory of it. Whatever happened and however we remember it—or can't—the residual feelings linger in the shadowy places. When this is triggered or emotional pain surfaces in our everyday lives—especially as anxiety, ambiguous responses, or overreactions—we might not understand these to be useful signals. These signals from obscured chasms indicate, definitively, that we need to attend to an open core wound in our inner lives. A wound within the high-walled ravine of safety and security, esteem and affection, or power and control needs attention.

This wounding is manifest in the whole person, not just emotionally and hidden out of view. Though we don't realize it, wounds compel us to stay protectively wedged in our ravines in two ways that keep us from fully healing: We keep unconsciously making decisions to avoid the feelings of associated pain. And we try to control or conquer these wound areas with the choices we make, how we interact with others, or the projects we take on. Either way, we hunker down within the ravine of that wound—often without even knowing it.

Remember Sarah, whose story we looked at in the beginning of this chapter? The original need, caused by financial and material deprivation, created emotional and spiritual peril. Challenging circumstances could have been made even worse if they were handled inappropriately by her caretakers within her childhood ecosystem. As an adult, even after she has plenty, she continues to compensate for this core wound. She will continue to somehow feel unsafe and insecure. Sarah will stay in need and in want until fully integrated healing occurs.

For some of us, the inner terrain relating to safety and security is only an occasional rough patch. For others, it remains the periodic steep valley. Still others are like Sarah, for whom the wound is a looming abyss that dominates many decisions and preoccupations each day.

Keating says that core wounds are what demand our attention and incite us to persist with "programs for happiness and fulfillment." The problem shows up early. Van der Kolk explains his findings on this kind of trauma. It causes both emotional and physiological effects: "Children who don't feel safe in infancy have trouble regulating their moods and emotional responses as they grow older. By kindergarten, many disorganized infants are either aggressive or spaced out and disengaged, and they go on to develop a range of psychiatric problems. They also show more physiological stress, as expressed in heart rate, heart rate variability, stress hormone responses, and lowered immune factors. Does this kind of biological dysregulation automatically reset to normal as a child matures or is moved to a safe environment? So far as we know, it does not."[2]

Is healing possible for Sarah? Yes. Often the discomfort must reach a point where reflecting on the landscape of her inner world is less frightening and painful than what she is experiencing in her daily life. When she's ready, she can explore what made her insecure, afraid, or ashamed as a child. She can encounter those feelings knowing she is strong enough to bear them, and she can give them the attention they deserve.

Sarah can realize how her efforts and projects are meant to heal something that won't ever heal that way. Wholeness will be found in reintegrating the separated pieces and settling down into what is more substantial and able to give her lasting peace. As she moves forward, it's best when this includes radical honesty and an authentic relationship with God. Add to that meaningful, ongoing spiritual practices that keep the landscape of the heart cultivated for the Divine Sower. Connected to God and connected to others, such practices will help sustain her and move her toward healing.

Esteem and Affection

The second chasm relates to an intermediate stage in human development. As we grow into young children, we come into greater awareness of the world outside our own immediate needs for security and safety. At this point, a sense of an independent self develops. At a certain point in young children's lives, they develop a working "theory of mind"—that is, they begin to understand that their thoughts are their own and that other people have different ideas and desires. For instance, they keenly know the difference between "mine" and "yours," especially if someone takes their favorite toy.

The differentiation goes deeper for the interior life. Along with a notion of a separate self is also formed a kind of mutated offshoot. Children soon learn that they must act in certain ways, do certain things, and say certain words to be understood, appreciated, accepted, and even loved and cared for by the people around them. Author and Cistercian monk Father

Thomas Merton referred to this as a "false self." In the Johari Window, this is quadrant 2: the facade quadrant. Sometimes it includes quadrant 4—the unknown quadrant—if we are behaving in certain ways unknowingly.

When we reach adolescence, we start having a pressing concern of a different kind. It takes up a lot of energy in terms of mental and emotional bandwidth. Routinely, we imagine what other people are thinking about us. By this point, many of us derive personal value not just from external rewards but from our internal interpretations of those rewards. That is, the wounded part of us perceives what those looking on must be feeling and thinking about us. We then may assume that they are making judgments about us and our worth. For adolescents, these perceptions become overbearing and warped all too quickly, and they can beleaguer us for years beyond adolescence—sometimes for decades or perhaps an entire lifetime.

This is the chasm of esteem and affection. We construct a false self to deal with this wound and the other chasms. "The (destructive) ego is the false self—born out of fear and defensiveness," explains spiritual writer John O'Donohue.[3] When our wounds are activated, our false selves are always neurotic. Thus the false self functionally obscures your deepest core, even from yourself. We begin to believe the fiction we initiated, or we begin to feel even more confused and irritated by the discrepancy.

In contrast, our authentic selves are the places where we can most purely sense God's love and grace for us and then extend our compassion toward others. As our authentic selves become obscured, we may feel a growing alienation from ourselves and from others. We may feel lost, alone, and like a misfit. We may feel like we need to "find ourselves." It takes time and effort to unlearn our typical reactions that are responses out of woundedness. We need to peel back the unnecessary layers of the false self to see all the beauty hiding underneath—the self that we've been afraid is too fragile to be exposed.

To give needed balance to this insight, theologian and writer Cynthia Bourgeault points out that we can make an error by assuming that the false self is some inextricable part of the human condition that is diseased.[4] We can wrongly surmise that this part of us is evidence of damage or pathology—something that should be cured or rooted out. While our false selves can become problematic or distorted, it is part of the entire organism of us. Our false selves can be integrated in certain ways to work in harmony and within our normal functioning so we can navigate our lives. Tact, diplomacy, and professionalism are potential ways for us to engage some aspects of our false selves in healthy and helpful ways. Indeed, spiritual healing and transformation allow us to not defeat this ego-fueled false self so much as transcend it.[5] The wounded ego is healed when the landscape of the heart is cultivated and the fruit of the Spirit prevails upon it.

How can we know if we've activated a wound that engages our false selves? We start by noticing when we are in discomfort. Notice if you start feeling annoyed, upset, or somehow triggered. Are you having judgmental, uncompassionate, petty, or malicious thoughts? Are you saying words or doing deeds with those attitudes? Other ways to tell are when we catch ourselves trying to feel validated or trying to look impressive, smart, or accomplished to others. It is then when we know we are maneuvering from headquarters erected in this interior chasm of a wound.

At times, our false selves work like magnets and attract others with the same issues. We might team up with others for solidarity and form a "wounded clique." If you sense the caustic chasm atmosphere, resist the urge to commiserate. Grace allows for insecurities and imperfections but doesn't abide by unkindness. Let's make sure we try to add vitality and empowerment in a group through encouragement to keep our social environments healthy. We can also create limits on the time we spend with people who are having trouble in the same ravine so it doesn't become an area of deeper damage.

Have you noticed your false self showing up lately? Mine surfaces each day, at least in some little irritating way. Give yourself a chance to think through a recent ordinary day. How many times did you consider what other people think about you and how you would be perceived? How many times did you try to seem a certain way? Did you long to seem smart, impressive, upstanding, or kind? These actions all harken back to the inner ravine of esteem and affection and trying to soothe the core wound.

If it feels like middle school or high school never ended, that is a signpost that you're stuck in this chasm. I've noticed that if I'm with others in new surroundings, this core wound can emerge for me—and sometimes I can observe it in others as well. Certain events or circumstances can jab these tender and wounded inner places, and our conversations and mind frames suffer for it.

Since our false selves can be comforting and familiar to us, it can be disconcerting to think of who we will be apart from it. Cultivating wholeness means transfiguration, not death, of the false self. Divine Love casts out fear and embraces our full selves.

Remember Norman? Healing for Norman will likely require him to be brave as he notices and retools how he relates to others. His tendency to overidentify himself and his worth with what he does for others means he will need to decide what boundaries are important for him and how he will set them up. As of now, he craves far more than ordinary amounts of affirmation; he knows little about himself apart from other people's expectations and the emotional enmeshments he creates or maintains with others. Instead of trying to prove himself worthy of love, Norman will need to get acquainted with being comfortable without performing. He can begin accepting and nourishing his identity as God's beloved child and "doing nothing." Without the outside pressures, he can reorient his perceptions and his path. Norman can create more opportunities for self-care and avoid or balance situations and relationships that don't allow him enough self-efficacy.

Power and Control

The third chasm is mighty, and it seems to occupy plenty of inner terrain for almost every adult person alive. It can form during the tender years of childhood or show up after trauma. This is the ravine of power and control. It is the core wound from which stems many of the global problems plaguing humankind throughout history too. We use enormous energies and programs to maintain order as we operate from this inner gorge. We employ countless tactics to control our surroundings and create certain outcomes. The more fearful and insecure we are, the deeper this ravine can feel. If you had little control in your life as a child, this area of your inner world may be highly problematic.

Entire industries and technologies have been fashioned to give us a powerful dashboard-style life. A touchscreen, a camera, a readout, a notification reminder: these things make us feel more powerful and make our days seem easier to control.

Remember J leaving home? J left one situation of powerlessness to enlist in another that would also control their life. The military ordered J to do whatever, whenever, and however and then shipped J off to an assignment with little warning. This is a very common plight for people with this wound. In the process of acting unconsciously, we can choose situations again and again that are very similar to the ones we are trying to be rid of. When we don't have the insights to do any better, we can put ourselves in the same kind of bind and end up having to figure out the problem once again.

For J, healing looks like taking the time to reflect on the wounds of their upbringing. Some good skills may have been learned at home, like the ability to be responsible for others, but J may have lost their childhood and sense of agency. A time of grief and lament will be needed. Without proper reflection, people with similar issues sometimes revert to times of being childish and irresponsible. They may launch into rebellious phases that were skipped during their upbringings, or they may treat their bodies unwisely because they are exercising their power to choose before they notice what is influencing their needs to soothe their core wounds. Healing will involve gaining clarity on the hidden influences and learning to not live reactively. J would be helped by the accompaniment of a trained professional and someone who could understand their predisposition to create codependent relationships, sink back into situations of disempowerment, or overreact and become controlling in all sorts of ways that are unhelpful and fear-based. Spiritual practices that allow J to center down and listen to their authentic self and to listen to God's Spirit will form a truer compass to guide J toward healthier ways of being.

A propensity to plan, anxious micromanaging, passive-aggressive maneuvers in relationships, trying to fix others, obsessive list-making, exasperation when expectations aren't met: these are all symptoms of a life lived in this chasm wound of power and control. Which ones do you have? The ravine of power and control influences so many of our actions and reactions each day that it's likely we fail to comprehend its actual influence.

Living with fear and uncertainty is uncomfortable, and seeking control is often our default coping mechanism. It is a normal part of pursuing equilibrium in our lives. As we begin to notice the core wounds we have, let's remember that being aware is the beginning of the Spirit's work in us. We can further invite the Spirit to till this chasm ground within so we can heal and find renewed ways of living, interacting, and moving toward wholeness.

What to Do When You Notice a Core Wound

Being uncomfortable or triggered is an indication that you have engaged a core wound. Triggers that incite various emotional states may come from responses to our conditions, circumstances, or remembered or perceived threats. These may start as subjective feelings and sometimes lead to thoughts and behavior.[6] This begins *below* our conscious level of awareness. After this point, the brain will begin to construct meaning. The brain functions as the architect of our experiences and emotions as it proceeds to organize all the information and input coming at us from our world. It is the organ that is extremely good at finding patterns, making predictions, sensing threats, and synthesizing sensory inputs.[7] When we try to survive agonizing circumstances, our brains will often cut off bodily senses from our conscious perceptions. But this emergency maneuver only works momentarily.

When unmitigated, injuries triggered in the inner world perpetuate distress and stall spiritual growth. Unhealed wounds will continue to dictate our lives and many decisions we make. They block our efforts to find fulfillment and satisfaction. They keep us from loving and being loved fully. The loving regard of the Divine allows for healing.

Reintegrating the hurt and fearful sensations of the nonlingual "feeling mind" that allow for the incorporation with the language center and conscious part of the mind is the only thorough and bodily way to find lasting healing and composure. "Because traumatized people often have trouble sensing what is going on in their bodies, they lack a nuanced response to frustration," says van der Kolk. "They either react to stress by becoming 'spaced out' or with excessive anger. Whatever their response, they often can't tell what is upsetting them. This failure to be in touch with their bodies contributes to their well-documented lack of self-protection and high rates of re-victimization and also to their remarkable difficulties feeling pleasure, sensuality, and having a sense of meaning."[8]

To start healing from early core wounds, begin to feel reconnected with your bodily senses again. If feeling numb, closed off, or disassociated from your body is a problem for you, then you've probably gotten good at shutting things out or shutting down emotions or sensations. To start to mend, begin to take better notice of your body through a careful noticing of all the parts of you.

Try this method: Lie down somewhere comfortable, and do a slow scan of awareness for your whole body. Start at the top of your head, and ask yourself if you sense pain, discomfort, or any sensation. Then move down to each part of your body. You should notice sensations as you pay greater attention. It may take practice or several tries to figure it out. Areas of tightness, pain, or other sensations may come into your awareness. Don't be afraid of what you feel. Re-member and welcome yourself back together. Focus on slow, deep breaths that draw you back to a feeling of wholeness. Keep track of your growing ability to reconnect your awareness to parts of your body that ache or feel pain. Notice how the whole organism of you feels in different situations when you scan it at other times. More information and practical help related to healing and wholeness are coming in later chapters.

The spiritual practices you will read about in this book can start the process of healing. If it feels overwhelming to approach your inner world, ask honest questions, or feel what arises in your body, then seek out some help. It will be most wise to seek professional help from a trauma-based therapist or trained spiritual director who specializes in trauma issues. Indeed, you may find that as you encounter some of these wounds through your reading or in the spiritual practices sections in this book, you can no longer "go it alone" in this process. Find someone with training who can hold space for the pain or discomfort you are feeling without trying to move you to pleasant emotions quickly. When someone helping you hasn't done their own full exploration of the land within, the process of hearing your pain will trigger their own discomfort, making them far less helpful at walking with you.

In the next chapter, we will learn a paradigm-shifting perspective to help us relate wisely and more objectively to our thoughts and feelings. Using specific wisdom from Desert Father Evagrius Ponticus and others, we will learn to witness the weather in our wild lands within.

Spiritual Practice: Sensory Accounting

This practice invites you to prayerfully consider the three chasms of safety and security, esteem and affection, and power and control in your life and to identify wounds in each of these ravines. Make efforts to notice your correlating bodily tension, pain, or any sensations associated with remembering wounds from those areas.

Respond to these questions:

1. In what ways in your early childhood did you feel unsafe or fearful? If you can remember an instance or two, jot down notes. Imagine for several undivided moments what the little child in you felt like while being powerless and afraid. Notice in all the places in your body where you have tension, pain, or sensation. Common places include the jaw, temples, neck, chest, shoulders, stomach, toes, and other places. Scan your body and make note of these.

2. In what ways did you long for affection, appreciation, or belonging in your childhood and adolescence? When did you feel like a misfit or "not enough"? Write down your thoughts. Acknowledge those wounds as real, important, and valid. Then notice how your body has held this pain. Common places are the neck, shoulders, head, jaw, chest, solar plexus, abdomen, fingers and toes, and many other places in the body. Take notes on what you find.

3. In what ways have you not had power and control in your life? A circumstance, an authority figure, a personal issue? Note the ways in which this happened. Many times these memories coincide with sensations like an area of tightness or constriction in the body. Other times, there are deeper pains, nausea, bruised places, and heavy or achy spots. Make a note of where you feel these sensations showing up bodily.

    In what ways do you try to keep power and control over your life now? For instance, do you make lists? Do you ever act in passive-aggressive ways? Do you have any anxious or hypervigilant behaviors? Any disordered eating, substance issues, or other habits? Do you procrastinate? What else do you do to feel in more control? There is no judgment here. Remind yourself that you are just taking a personal inventory, as objectively as possible, to understand yourself more deeply. Note the ways that you try to ensure that you can control your life and have power over it.

4. If you feel comfortable, offer this prayer now that you are beginning to explore your difficult inner terrain:

> God, I am noticing my inner self and my body in new ways as I recall pain and things from long ago. Soothe me with your Spirit and give me the courage to feel what I cut off from myself to survive during difficult times so I might move toward wholeness. Thank you for calling me into a deeper kind of life. I commit my whole self to you. Amen.

5

WEATHER FRONTS

Witnessing Our Afflicting Thoughts

The land within us has weather, and it's time to learn what that means. Climate on earth is the larger system in which we inhabit—in meteorological terms, it's a thirty-year average of weather conditions. Weather is the particular day-to-day combination of things such as air pressure, temperature, and precipitation. We've all encountered days of bad weather outside. What do we do about the wild weather that moves through our interior landscapes?

In chapter 2, we learned about desert elder Evagrius Ponticus, who lived in Egypt in the late fourth century and devoted much time to prayer. He can serve as a kind of professor of internal meteorology, teaching us to understand the confusing jumble of pressure systems moving through our inner landscapes. The best-known teachings of Evagrius come from a short book entitled *Praktikos*. In about one hundred brief sections, *Praktikos* helps ascetics live out a holy life in a setting of scant resources.[1] Here Evagrius teaches that the "afflicting thought" is what leads to the problems of sin. Professor Andrew Louth incisively phrases Evagrius's notion as "cracks in the heart."[2] These vulnerabilities are what make us susceptible to sin. Simply put, mortals have frailties. It's our weaknesses that incline us to errant lapses and sin.

As a spiritual guide, Evagrius taught his students that with God's help, they could renew their minds to—hopefully—avert sin altogether. Afflicting thoughts roll in like foul weather within the conditions of our particular inner climates. In and of themselves, these thoughts are not evil or sinful, and they need not harm our souls; depending on how we interact with them, however, we might suffer trouble or damage. He warns that we must be vigilant about temptations that might stir up our passions and beleaguer us.[3]

Evagrius advises us on eight particular afflicting thoughts, which we will examine in this chapter. The Greek word he used for "afflicting thought" is *logísmoi*, which means "thought rut." Before these "thought ruts" have an emotional charge connected to us, they do not have any power and are morally neutral, says Evagrius. Once we attach ourselves to them, however, these thoughts become destructive desires, fixations, troubles, or sins. We can be witnesses to them and not beholden to them. Even though we can't control incoming weather, we can see it on the horizon moving in. We can make wise clothing choices before going outdoors, or we can decide to shelter in place until after the front passes through.

Before we contend with our inner weather, however, Evagrius tells us that we have something else to handle first. The primary affliction to deal with, prior to considering the eight afflicting thoughts, is the love of self. This refers to self-ishness and self-preoccupation. We trample others as we push toward our goals, desires, and ambitions and center ourselves in our stories. We lose our souls in the process. If we are the center, then God is not. Evagrius was insistent: first, we must dispatch the treacherous love of self!

For Evagrius, the goal is not to subdue the weather of these afflicting thoughts. Neither does he train us to fear the weather or hide from it. After we first consider each of the eight weather patterns that pass through the wild land within, we will look further into Evagrius's insights about how to approach the weather patterns in general.

1. Gluttony

The first temptation occurs when the desert ascetic is hungry and thirsty: the temptation is to gorge on food and drink. The tendency in this situation, Evagrius warns, is to fixate on the hunger pains or sensations of thirst and to think that something dire is happening. He cautions his students to be careful when the focus on food or drink becomes a repeated preoccupation that distracts from prayer. Trouble begins when thoughts of eating and drinking become compulsive and disruptive enough that the monastic goes off course and violates the devotional commitments of simple living.

If you are not living the ascetic life right now, you probably aren't longing for food or drink in the same way. The afflicting thought of gluttony, as Evagrius writes about it, doesn't apply to you perfectly. But gluttonous afflicting thoughts have a modern counterpart that is routinely problematic. Gluttony—in Greek, *gastrimargía*—became associated with overindulgence when Pope Gregory the Great added it to the list of seven deadly sins. His teachings were for the church at large and applied to people both inside and outside of monastic life.

Indeed, Pope Gregory used the writings of Evagrius as a template for his own work on the seven deadly sins, also called the capital vices or cardinal sins. From his decidedly Western lens, Pope Gregory focused more on identifying wrongdoings and less on forecasting the weather of the inner life and preventing its sinful effects. He considered the sins ensuing from the eight afflicting thoughts as serious moral failings in need of confession and penance. Instead of cautionary wisdom, too often the seven deadly sins have been weaponized against people. Christians throughout history have been prone to use them as tools of judgment rather than redemptive aids.

Gluttony today, in terms of regular overeating and over-consuming, can lead to spiritual malformation. Habitually consuming in excess will never be healthy mentally or physically, but gluttony is a deeper issue. Gluttony is larger than the consumption of food and drink—it can involve compulsive desires to accumulate, binge on, or collect things as well. Gluttony shifts the focus from God and God's provision to our own appetites and serves to placate our fears of scarcity.

The virtue that counterbalances gluttony is charity. As we practice charity through generosity, we can move with intention through the terrain and climate conditions of scarcity, then we can be freed from gluttony. We may understand the seven other afflicting thoughts in the same way—as counterbalanced by a virtue.

2. Lust or Fornication

Because ascetics in the desert were celibate, many were tempted by longing for intimate physical connection and sexual relations. (Duh, right?) At the time, sexual intercourse, even within the bounds of marriage, was thought of as distinctly carnal and too distracting from spiritual pursuits and a devoted religious life. Desert monastics often struggled with lust when remembering what their sexual lives were like before they left for the wilderness, or their afflicting thoughts would tempt them to violate their commitment to stay chaste.

Generally, lust is connected with unbridled sexual desires and preoccupations. The Greek word for lust is *porneía* from the word *porneuo*, and it's the source of our English word *pornography*. In the Bible, porneía is often used metaphorically to speak of worshiping idols. It is used also when referring to engaging in or indulging in the whole range of sexual lust or sexual activities. The afflicting thoughts will arrive most certainly, but it is our involvement with them that creates the problems. If we are inattentive to them, they pass.

The virtue that counterbalances lust is chastity, which is also known as self-restraint. The ascetics knew and meditated on the words of Jesus from the Sermon on the Mount. Inspired by the beatitudes, they set their course to accomplish what Jesus proffered: "The pure in heart will see God." Remember from chapter 2 that the *heart* here is referring not to the emotional seat of the person but to the core of our beings? When the control center from which decisions and behavior emerge is uncontaminated, God is unobscured to us. When our cores are unadulterated, we can also hear and perceive how to live better.

When we know beforehand that the weather of lust is sure to blow through, we are prepared to stay uncorrupted and uncompromised at the command center of our lives. Our commitments can be kept, and there is no need to pretend that we are never tempted. We can build checks and balances and other methods of accountability and assistance into our lives. We can live with honest confession and transparency when the normal occurrences like the afflicting thoughts of lust emerge. What we choose to do about lust or any of the thought ruts reveals how much we are allowing the Spirit to work in us.

3. Avarice

Avarice, or love of money, is sometimes misunderstood as being tempted to be miserly, to hoard, or to be greedy. Although all those *are* eventually sins, as they withhold essentials from the needy, what Evagrius is warning about is something different. The afflicting thought of avarice that Evagrius focuses on—one that can lead to distraction from prayer and eventual sin—is actually more foundational to our ways of being. In Greek, *philaguría* relates to the worry about finances.[4]

A common concern among those in the desert setting was, "Will I be able to get by?" or "How will I manage when I get old, and who will take care of me?" Remember that because of their commitment to celibacy, some of the ascetics did not have children who could care for them when they were elderly. Their commitment to poverty meant too that they could not pay for caretakers in their final years.

Financial concerns are common today, as many of us wonder if we will have enough. Life is uncertain, and we deeply desire to feel secure. Because these thoughts can trigger common core wounds of safety and security and of power and control within all of us, thought ruts can grow into avarice. *Will God really provide everything, or will I be in desperate need?* we might think. A scarcity mentality creates an anxious life. These persistent questions can grow into compulsive worries that we try to remedy on our own in actions of desperation rather than moving along with God in a posture of trust.

This afflicting thought was later changed to the sin of greed in the seven deadly sins as outlined by Pope Gregory. Like a storm can lead to a flood or a mudslide, avarice can lead to other things too, like envy, despair, wrath, and hopelessness.

There is no magic trick or simple answer to snap us out of avarice, but a long walk in the right direction makes a big difference. A few practices, if done regularly, can give us perspective and protection from the bad weather of avarice. Challenge your presumptions or unchecked notions about sufficiency. Question and disrupt them regularly. Be generous, even when it feels uncomfortable. Ordinary practices of generosity can thwart the weather of avarice from seeping into your perspective and warping your sense of reality. If we let in unconscious false assumptions that God is limited and has limited resources, avarice will afflict us.

4. Dejection or Sadness

This afflicting thought is perhaps most accurately described as debilitating nostalgia. For the ascetic, memories of a better or easier life can keep one from staying in the present moment, or offering focused prayers, or being grateful. Everyone gets sad. But ongoing dejection—in Greek, *lúpe*—hampers spiritual maturity. When preoccupied by thoughts of one's former way of life as a better one, the ascetic will be diverted from growing in intimacy with God.

Just like the early desert monastics, we can persistently think of the past or the future. This will create discontentment and low spirits, and it will hinder our spiritual progress too. Learning to want what we have and to be where we are—even when it gets boring or troublesome—is a test of our mettle. Character development and spiritual maturity come not through times of pleasure and ease but from learning fortitude and faith during demanding times.

Evagrius knew that becoming aware of the predictable sadness that comes during tedious expanses of the day, activities we dislike, and arduous situations is actually good preparation for standing firm through trials. Focusing on the present moment—not longing for the past or being distracted by the future—and sensing that God is with us in this very moment is to focus on the truest reality available to us.

Years after Evagrius's work, Pope Gregory the Great took components of both this afflicting thought and *acedia*, which we will look at soon, and exchanged them for a new category called *sloth* in his list of seven deadly sins. He saw that sadness could acquire paralyzing and selfish features, which could create sins of omission and inactivity. In these cases, the self, not God, is the center of one's world, and one can't be bothered to do what's needed to be faithful and fruitful.

Once again, it is good to remember that sadness and dejection themselves are not sinful, according to Evagrius. They are ordinary human feelings that blow in from time to time. These feelings will soon spoil our day and our progress when we give them extra power through our attentions. The sadness weather soon soaks us and keeps us soggy. Giving ourselves the grace to notice these feelings, understand them, and accept them for what they are—without shame or condemnation—can help us deal with them promptly and honestly and then bid them goodbye. Ignoring them, stuffing them down, or running from them keep us unaware, and therein may be a storm system that will circle us for too long.

5. Wrath

The fieriest afflicting thought is a "boiling stirring up of wrath," says Evagrius.[5] This repetitive thought can be related to a past offense, real or imagined. He warns that wrath can thoroughly irritate the soul and seize the mind. It can grow into paranoia with its ability to distract and harm.[6]

Wrath—in Greek, orgé—is also called anger, and it is a normal and common human emotion. We need not feel guilty about experiencing anger. It can arise automatically and reflect both normal and unhealthy places within us. We may notice an injustice like police brutality and feel enraged. We may feel slighted by the betrayal of a friend and experience anger. This initial emotional response is not sinful. The apostle Paul cautions us, "In your anger do not sin. Do not let the sun go down while you are still angry" (Ephesians 4:26). Paul does *not* say, "Do not feel angry." Rather, he urges action to contend with the occurrences of anger directly. Do not embrace it like a weapon; do not add a log to its fire.

As I grew up, plenty of influential Christian people told me that anger is a sin. But that's like saying getting hurt or upset is a sin. This is a terribly damaging teaching. Instantaneous feelings that arrive within us are not sin. They are part of how we react to, cope with, and comprehend our world. What we decide to do with emotions can be either negative or positive, sinful or blessed. As we learn to notice and reflect on our instantaneous reactions, we can learn to do right by what is happening.

Because anger fires up so hot, however, it can indeed be dangerous. If it goes outward, it can become destructive. Or if we shove the fire down deep, it can act like subterranean volcanic pressure. Lava can flow through the landscape from active places of deep fire, or it can harden on the surface, into mesas of numbness and insensitivity. It's important to look carefully to see if anger has developed terrain qualities of its own. Common qualities of unexamined and entrenched anger include bitterness, mistrust, self-hate, depression, hopelessness, cynicism, and even misplaced guilt. Go to those places. Find the source, or dig past the hardened ground of anger to the deeper issues and core wounds.

Let us also be aware that in our society, there are unspoken rules, or social mores, for different people when it comes to anger. Expressions of anger are tolerated and even admired in certain people and not others. When people outside the socially dominant group express anger, the emotion is usually viewed as negative and even as a character flaw. This can create additional collateral damage within us who are marginalized.

It's possible to transfigure anger in healthy ways. No matter what gender we are or what color our skin, the problems associated with anger are best helped by perspective, space, and patience. Most importantly, *always ask your anger questions.* What hurts? What is threatened right now? What is my fear? Defensiveness about your own anger is also anger. Continually be very curious about your anger or defensiveness because it has so much to tell you about your hidden world.

If we find ourselves habitually irritated, angry, or annoyed, it's time to take inventory of our unresolved and unhealed pains and the disappointments that have made us afraid or caustic. Our emotions and behaviors are signals to alert us. Ask yourself, What has me feeling fiery, out of control, frustrated, or hurt?

Evagrius warns that unheeded anger turns into paranoia. Recent scientific studies back him up. Because the brain functions in pattern-finding, meaning-making ways, it predictively interprets meaning to save energy and time. Staying angry keeps us on red alert for threats and dangers, but it also makes it more likely that we will interpret our world incorrectly as being more dangerous and threatening than it is. This vigilance takes enormous amounts of personal energy, and it distracts us from being centered in God, who restores our souls. We find our best solace in God, not in our anger or vigilance. Higher amounts of the stress hormones cortisol and epinephrine, which are useful to get us to act in emergencies, overrelease in the body when we stay angry.

Wrath can come to us like a thunderstorm with gusty winds—a supercell in our inner worlds can spin off other storm cells quickly. It takes a lot of practice and awareness to rein in wrath if it's been common in your interior climate. Keep a careful eye out for it, and do what you can to prepare for it and deescalate it. When anger is mishandled, we can further distance ourselves from our pains and become disassociated within.

6. *Acedia*

I find *acedia*—otherwise known as despondency or listlessness—to be one of the most intriguing and prominent afflicting thoughts today. Remarkably, Evagrius noticed that this one reaches full potency between the hours of 10:00 a.m. and 2:00 p.m. He claimed that it makes the day seem fifty hours long. In the desert, acedia (Greek, *akedía*) was commonly called the "noonday demon" because it attacked people at their weakest moment: during the hottest time of the day when nothing amusing was happening.[7] Acedia can accumulate into other troubles—like sadness, dejected nostalgia, anxiety, and frustration—and then expand into sins of sloth or wrath.

One day, an ascetic might start out with what we might call "a case of the blahs" during a boring stretch of the morning. But then things would fester into irritating restlessness. When everything seemed dull, prayer could become tiresome, and then boredom or exasperation would set in. An ascetic might grow agitated and feel powerless too.

We've all been there—maybe while waiting for an important occasion, or during a monotonous meeting or class in school, or while moving through an extended project after the shine has long worn off. We want to shrug off our situations and move on instead of toughing them out and remaining committed.

In this case, we can better understand an afflicting thought by looking at its opposite. We can better understand acedia by going in the opposite direction for a moment: to worship. In worship, we are self-forgetting. Worship can often bring us toward heights of joy or relief. Why? Because for a time, we stop a certain kind of thinking in which we are planted and functioning at the center of our own worlds. In contrast, our attention and adoration during worship move outward to our Maker and Sustainer. This sets things back in order. For me, when "put in my right place," as it were, the focus of my attention is not on my desire. In substance, acedia is the opposite of self-forgetting and spiritual joy.

Plenty of acedia is observable in ourselves and our peers, though we might never realize it as such. For some, acedia might be experienced as spiritual torpor, characterized by listlessness, ennui, fatigue, and a lack of interest in matters that we used to find satisfying. In Latin, the word *acedia* is the same as the word for "negligence." Left unabated, acedia can make our outcomes negligent ones because we abandon our best efforts. In the weather system of acedia, we might experience low energy. We may sense our own aimlessness or feel our determination dwindling. This inner weather can make us question our decisions and commitments. We may grow discontented.

Certain cultures can make this weather front of acedia worse. In the United States, for instance, there is much focus on individualism: finding our true callings and pursuing our desires and dreams. So we may think that our paths should be filled with excitement and satisfaction. Doing anything well—schooling, parenting, acquiring an athletic or musical skill, creating a useful product, writing a book—almost always takes time and effort. Sometimes working for something bigger than ourselves softens the weather of acedia. Yet when building an organization, business, or ministry, we can go through years of restless feelings and discouragement and the sense that we have little to show for our efforts. Acedia thought ruts will always contend for our attention. Whether it comes to us at noon or at another time of day or night, acedia is powerful and pernicious.

When we attach to the afflicting thoughts of acedia, we are not able to live in the moments where our lives are taking place. Instead, we are removed to the past or another place. Like many, I have struggled with acedia, at first not knowing it had a name or specific characteristics. Learning that acedia is part of the normal weather of the inner world—and that it is especially common when we are engaged in things that require care, time, and discipline—was a relief. When these feelings and thoughts roll in now, I can see them for what they are and carry on.

When this weather hits, I like to ask, Am I doing anything to make this weather seem worse than it actually is? If I dwell on times other than what is at hand and if my focus is sharply on keeping myself entertained, I know my acedia will be heightened and prolonged. Acedia fools us into thinking that fantasy or unreality is preferable to the present situation. But these delay tactics eventually make us more discontented. It also helps me to have encouragement from others in the same situations and to know that people have endured the same kind of acedia or even worse. Cultivating wholeness, for the desert elders, meant weathering the acedia and trusting that it would eventually pass as they allowed God to be their joy and strength.

7. Vainglory

Like a subtle low-pressure system that eases onto our landscapes first as very pleasant weather, vainglory glides in. Only after a while does it suck the air out of the place, making it hard to breathe.

Some of us might remember being reprimanded as children if we were caught boasting or bragging. Being reserved about our accomplishments, our smarts, and our possessions or blessings was the only appropriate behavior. Especially in previous decades, gloating or showing off was not tolerated. I don't remember this problem referred to as vainglory (in Greek, *kenodoxía*), but that is the name for it. Evagrius teaches that vainglory is a prevalent afflicting thought.

The "vain" part of vainglory refers to the temporary and insubstantial nature of the activity or thought. Trying to get "glory" that is self-centered is pointless and worthless, taught Evagrius. Showing off gives us diminishing returns and creates negative spiritual consequences that distract us from developing Christlikeness.

With vainglory, it is the attachment to the social reward component that creates a troubling shift. Evagrius warned that this temptation comes *after* most of the other afflicting thoughts are weathered. At a certain point, when we've managed to put our lives in order and create consistent, righteous habits, we are then tempted to peacock about how good we've been doing.

Evagrius knew the frailties of the human condition very well. He knew that our deep longings for acceptance and admiration quickly distract us from lives devoted to God as the true Source of our fulfillment. Through little mistakes of vainglory, we begin to love the attention and adoration of others—and not just love it but yearn for it, attach to it, grow to demand it, learn how to procure it, and then, of course, feel dejected without it. Evagrius warned his students about the fantasies that often arise within secluded religious life in particular. These disciples would be tempted with desires to be the most righteous, the most devoted, the most talented, the smartest, and the most accomplished—and even the humblest. Vainglory afflicts the pious, the "do-gooders," and religious people with the most stealth. Because doing good often doesn't come with extrinsic rewards like money, possessions, or power, we are instead tempted to subtly signal others to our moral or spiritual proficiencies.

With the advent of social media, most of us could qualify for expert-level badges in vainglory. Social media companies like Facebook, Instagram, Twitter, Snapchat, and others rely on vainglory for their very existence. People touting their virtue is what makes billions of social media users feel validated, and it can seem perfectly harmless. Now billions of dollars are at stake if we *aren't* vainglorious.

Vainglory, when it's used against others in public or social settings, also looks like judgmentalism or cancel culture. When we point out the mistakes, faults, and poor character of someone else, we draw vainglorious distinctions between them and ourselves, or "us good guys." If someone lacks goodness, good sense, or piety, will we tell everyone about it?

Along with acedia, vainglory is one of the most insidious afflicting thoughts of our cultural milieu. Most of us are unaware of it. Too many times I've caught myself considering how I might capture some occurrence in my day and place it into a post that could reflect well on me. Maybe it was the kind way I helped someone or the money I sent somewhere. The truth is, I've wanted other people to admire me. On the surface, maybe it doesn't seem so bad. In our culture now, it's completely normalized. Though it's normal, we must ask ourselves, Does doing it make us more like Jesus?

When you feel compelled to share something good that you've done, ask yourself, Is this hard to keep to myself because I'd like some credit for doing good? Am I trying to make a distinction between myself and someone else, and why is that so important to me right now? Who am I trying to impress right now, and why? If it's a routine thought pattern, then it points in some way to an esteem and affection core wound that needs our closer attention.

Here are two helpful ways to guard against vainglory: giving in secret (or doing good deeds anonymously or not telling anyone else about it) and cultivating a genuine attitude of ongoing modesty and restraint.

When we find sufficiency in God, then mining for the good opinions of others seems less attractive. Restraint in reiterating goodness and being reticent to get credit will come more easily.

The pressures to impress others with our virtues dissipate when we don't believe and behave as though others are holding the measuring stick.

Pope Gregory the Great did not include vainglory as one of seven deadly sins. He saw that the temptation of vainglory would be better expressed through the two serious sins of envy and pride, and he added both to his list of seven deadly sins instead. We turn lastly to pride.

8. Pride

When prideful, we have a working amnesia about the work of Divine Grace. Evagrius taught that the temptation to pride was not a core-level depravity, which is in contrast to how Western Christianity has understood it and what Pope Gregory taught. Evagrius taught that pride was delusional—a misperception of reality. Evagrius said pride comes to afflict us after all the other afflicting thoughts have reduced us. The sin of pride, then, happens when we've deteriorated and become consumed with other thoughts, problems, and sin. Pride (in Greek, *huper-ephanía*) is likened to a pathology of the mind by which we are rendered unreasonable and unreachable. In pride, our hearts are hardened from self-righteousness, and we can't realize that our humility is gone. We've become too unaware to apprehend the sorry state we're in.

Many of us have heard *grace* defined as "unmerited favor." That definition doesn't describe what *happens* as the power of grace changes our lives. Unmerited favor is experienced as the presence of God with us. Grace puts every single one of us on equal footing. This life-giving connection is what we discard when we sin in pride. When we become prideful, we take the position that grace must need to exist for others but not for us. This weather is some of the worst. Like a blizzard or torrents of rain, pride obscures everything. Self-satisfaction and smugness reveal that one is senselessly out of touch with reality, says Evagrius. This is a brilliant way of understanding spiritual sickness that needs true healing. If we don't learn how to watch for stormy weather, it can be ruinous.

Begin to Witness

Evagrius invites us into a paradigm shift. Rather than assuming we *are* simply gluttonous people, or lustful people, or angry people, we can understand instead that we may *experience* a gluttonous thought, or an angry thought, or a lustful thought. These afflicting thoughts, as we've learned, are a kind of weather front that sometimes moves through our wild lands within. Remember, we aren't the weather, and we don't own the weather; we let it pass. Evagrius's wisdom gives us great insight. He tells us that all our cravings can be *witnessed*. It is our compulsion to personally identify with temptation and to sin through these afflicting ways that keep us from being free.

By seeing temptations for what they are and by avoiding being swept into their forces, we don't have to capitulate to them. Though we may long for the things the afflicting thoughts tempt us with and be distracted by them at first, we can still retain self-control. Just like the Spirit guided Jesus, the Spirit guides us too. Another way to describe self-control is *self-possession*. To be self-possessed is to be possessed not by anything or anyone else. Rather than losing self-control, we are in possession of ourselves through the power of the Spirit. This is spiritual fruit.

Since the goal is to neither eradicate the weather of the afflicting thoughts nor fear it, nor hide from it, what does Evagrius advise? The wise disciple has what Evagrius calls *apatheia*. This word, on the surface, looks a bit like apathy. But its meaning is very different. Apatheia can be described as a state of calm, which is the prerequisite for love and knowledge.[8] The word is interchangeable with the phrase "wholeness of heart."

A person with apatheia is not controlled by fickle passions or inordinate attachments. If we have apatheia, we have a balanced kind of management system for running our lives, says author and Episcopal priest Cynthia Bourgeault.[9] In this state, negative circumstances are not given the emotional heft we once ascribed to them, and we are not carried away by our appetites or by matters that distract us from a life of love and devotion. A wise person is skilled in the maintenance of their inner world. They do not fixate on the material or the external, and they do not become swayed by social pressures or the pleasures prized in this world.

Evagrius advises that making wisdom manifest happens by taking on the nature of Christ through imitation and submission. This eventually results in an even-tempered disciple whose life is centered in God's ways and will. This is a life that bears the fruit of the Holy Spirit. Foundational to spiritual maturity and continued growth is being attuned with, and not hostile to, *reality* as it is—both within us and in the world.

In the 1500s in Spain, priest and theologian Ignatius of Loyola wrote of something quite similar, something he called "Holy Indifference." Holy Indifference is a sanctified, loosened grasp on the worries and stresses that are outside our control. It should not be confused with how we might typically understand the word *indifference*: as a lack of concern, interest, or sympathy. Rather, Holy Indifference is a God-given grace, a gift. It is not something that one attains by merit, inborn qualities, or diligence. Though we can't work for this gift, we can prepare ourselves to receive it. This happens best by the practice of surrendering, daily and in all things, to God. It is the practice of growing in grace that leads to Christlikeness.

When we have Holy Indifference, we are not mastered by our emotions or circumstances; rather, we wait on the Lord. It takes the prayer words of Jesus as words to live by: "Not my will, but Yours be done." We believe and behave as though we are dependent on God for each next step and for our ultimate strength. In practicing Holy Indifference, we let go of the expectations that disappoint us and of the notion that we must control every unfolding turn and twist in our lives. The ego—which I'm referring to here as a pattern of self-interested and self-referential thoughts—is disempowered with the gift of Holy Indifference.

Apatheia gives us the strength and durability for equipoise: the act of balance. It lends stability for the storms that test us and the sunny days that can make us complacent. Holy Indifference is a function of the soul's resiliency. This is how we weather the land within.

The Prayer of Quiet

To live lives of Holy Indifference, of apatheia, the desert elders would sink deeply and continually into what they called the "prayer of quiet." This type of prayer is called *apophatic* prayer. It does not employ words. Apophatic prayer involves a mindful and relinquishing disposition in the process of communing with God. This contemplative method of praying does not use images, requests, intercessions, and rituals. It involves the quieting of one's spirit and the settling into the essence of being, which allows one to be found in the presence of God.

Many of us in Western contexts and cultures are accustomed to only word-based praying. We understand God mainly through an acquisition of knowledge that affirms what and who God is. This is the *kataphatic* way of knowing God. This is the first way we begin to know God (or anything, for that matter): with definitions, descriptions, concepts, categories, images, and words. After some development, we understand more fully that God is transcendent, uncontainable. We may notice that God shatters any box of mental understanding we have been misusing. Then we may come to a place that points beyond conceptions so that we may start to discover what God is not and allow room for what we can hardly conceive—God is no *thing*.

Sometimes other names can help disrupt our hardened and limited concepts of God: Divine Love, Mystery, Source. Apophatic theology, seen most fully within Eastern Orthodox Christianity, invites the spiritually devoted beyond limitations and known categories to ways that make room for what we don't know and cannot comprehend about the Divine. The prayer of quiet draws us ever deeper into the Mystery that is worth

growing familiar with but is ultimately unknowable in its totality. There is a boundlessness of the One who we, in English,
sometimes call God, and apophatic prayer may lead us into that
unknowing to experience the divine beyond what we know.

Cistercian monk Father Thomas Keating says, "The inner
dynamism of contemplative prayer leads naturally to the transformation of [our] whole personality. Its purpose is not limited to [our] moral improvement. It brings about a change in
[our] way of perceiving and responding to reality. This process
involves a structural change of consciousness."[10] The shift of
consciousness to which Keating speaks is initiated by the Spirit.
By settling into and being received by the transforming power
of Divine Love, we are changed. Contemplative prayer won't
transform you in a day, a week, or a year, but those whose lives
are ones of habitual surrender to God in stillness radiate the
presence of Christ.

Priest, theologian, professor, and author Henri Nouwen
wrote in his book *The Way of the Heart*,

> In the sayings of the Desert Fathers, we can distinguish
> three aspects of silence. All of them depend and strengthen
> the central idea that silence is the mystery of the future
> world:

> > First, silence makes us pilgrims.
> > Secondly, silence guards the fire within.
> > Thirdly, silence teaches us to speak.[11]

Weather Reports

Now is a good time to ask yourself, What is the weather within like lately? What storms have been rolling through? Look over all eight afflicting thoughts, and be honest about which thought ruts are most prominent. What are some ways you can keep a "weather log" to help you see your patterns of thoughts and feelings as passing weather fronts? How will you choose to witness each afflicting thought as it passes along instead of attaching to it? What greater insight about unknown places within you and what knowledge might God's Spirit be giving you? About your core wounds or about the climate zones, common weather, or the insufficient old maps that you've been using? Discussing these notes with your book club or small group or a spiritual companion will give you added insights and resolve.

In the next chapter, we will explore this contemplative way of intimacy with God that we have glimpsed so far. We will learn about the depths of silence, stillness, and solitude in aspects that are alien to our contemporary culture but provide our souls with nourishment.

Spiritual Practice: Practicing the Presence

The Bible tells us that God is Spirit: everywhere and always present. But often, we live like functional atheists because we don't incorporate this Reality as we live. This spiritual practice—practicing the presence—helps us *wake up* to God's continual presence by means of conversation and attendance.

We do this not just in a series of prayers but through a slow transformation into a life that becomes a prayer itself.

To adopt this practice, make a point of bringing a meaningful awareness of God's presence into your mind many times a day. As you pause to survey your internal weather, be in conversation with God in ordinary ways, as you would with a dear friend. Keep some record of how this continuing conversation is going and how it's changing you.

If this kind of awareness is foreign to you, you may want to start by adding some reminders or changing your typical atmosphere in small ways. Place some prompt notes for yourself in key spots around your house or office, wear a reminder rubber band on your wrist, or—my favorite—get an hourly chime app for your phone. When you see a prompt note, notice the rubber band on your wrist, or hear the chime, it's your reminder to prayerfully draw your attention to God.

In whatever way you are reminded, take a minute or so to refocus your attention and pray, "Holy One, I come into your divine presence and holiness. Let me remember that you are here." Do it as often as you can every single day to practice noticing the presence of God with you.

Revisit your queries. Go back to your responses to the Quaker queries at the end of chapter 1. As you revisit them, make notes about what you've learned. Then ask yourself the same queries and write down your new or updated responses.

STILL WATERS

Opening Ourselves within Prayer

I had been working with Julie for a few sessions as a spiritual companion. A vibrant woman and married mother of preschool-age twins, Julie was diligently finishing up her graduate degree in nursing. She was also very active in church ministry as well as in palliative hospice care. Julie asked me to journey with her, as she was having trouble finding her next steps and knowing what God wanted her to do. In prayer, we asked the Holy Spirit to guide the process.

After I got to know her and her situation a little better, as her spiritual companion, I asked her open-ended questions that might help her see her own life more clearly. Though she was extremely busy and trying hard in all aspects of life, she had been praying fervently and hoping that God would give her some signs. During the spiritual companioning process, she found purposeful ways she could start quieting down and encountering prayer besides the familiar forms of thanksgiving, petition, and intercession.

Soon after we started journeying together, Julie realized that what she needed most was to find more space and time to be quieter and still to hear from God. She decided to set apart times from her frenetic string of responsibilities. Instead of launching right into her list of prayer requests, she began to slow things down. First, she would light her favorite scented candle and try to find a relaxed rhythm of breathing for a few minutes. Then in a calmer state, she would read a portion of Psalms. After settling into this slower pace and quieter atmosphere, she would then spend a few minutes thinking about the Scripture while setting aside all her other thoughts. After being quiet with God for about five minutes, she would close the time in a prayer of thanksgiving.

She reconnected with me after a few weeks and seemed a little timid to tell me what happened.

"Was it a positive experience?" I asked.

"It was," Julie affirmed. "I've never experienced anything like it. But something has been happening, and I don't know why. I sort of feel weird talking about it," she added a bit hesitantly.

I waited a bit to see if she'd say more. Then I asked, "Are you crying a lot, once things get quiet?"

"Oh my gosh. How did you know?" she said smiling and exhaling with relief.

What Julie was experiencing—an abundance of tears when she began to enter spaces of quiet—is normal. The desert elders actually wrote about this. It is called by a few names: *the blessing of tears, the gift of tears,* or *holy tears.* Holy tears can occur as we allow the Spirit to work and our hearts become tenderer. Hardened things inside us that we don't even know are there become loosened and move to the surface of our knowing. This is good news.

I've had to explain the goodness of the gift of tears to more than a few people. I've noticed that most people assume something has gone wrong, or they worry that they are heading toward a debilitating emotional breakdown. Some are confused and frightened by the sudden influx of tears that is unlike ordinary weeping. It coincides with an experience of God's presence.

This infrequent blessing is a reintegration of our spirits and our bodies that takes place in a space beyond words. It is a grace of God and a kind of sacrament of love. At times, we are moved to tears in repentance and contrition over sin. But the gift of tears can be entwined in the process of healing our bodies, emotions, and spirits as we advance toward wholeness and sense the comfort of God.

I delight in how Psalm 23:1–3 gives us a picture of the land within us that is lush and restful. We can be shepherded to this place. Since sheep are defenseless animals that get easily alarmed, they are too nervous to drink from fast-moving or noisy streams. They want calm water and peaceful places to graze. When we are ready, the Spirit of God guides us gently to these places for refreshment. And it is at the quiet green pastures near the still waters that, like Julie, we may find comfort and the gift of tears.

The Contemporary English Version (CEV) translation of the Bible provides a beautiful picture of what our inner landscapes can be under the direction of such a kind Shepherd:

You, Lord, are my shepherd.
I will never be in need.
You let me rest in fields of green grass.
You lead me to streams of peaceful water, and you
    refresh my life.

Finding these tranquil streams means waiting in inner stillness for God to lead us. Sometimes we act more like goats, clopping off on our own and climbing up high onto the crevices of our ravines. We'll precariously teeter on our hooves instead of joining the movements of the Shepherd toward the reviving and peaceful waters. When we finally relent and find what God has for us, we may find ourselves overcome with joy and relief. We might not have the language for it, but the deep parts of ourselves may respond, and the outpouring can be the blessing of tears.

The man who is often called the father of monks, Anthony of Egypt, said, "If a person loves God with all their heart, all their thoughts, all their will, and all their strength, they will gain reverence of God; the reverence will produce tears, tears will produce strength; by the perfection of this the soul will bear all kinds of fruits."[1] In those moments of yielding in quiet before the Divine, we glimpse divine intimacy. The tears may come. If this happens to you during spiritual practices or experiences, you're in good company. You are beginning to unwrap the gifts within the contemplative stream of spirituality. From the ground of *being* and silence, the holy work happens.

Let's now see how God invites us to more as we sync our paces to the pace of Divine Love. When our cores, our spirits, become centered down, as Howard Thurman writes, we begin to open up to God in vital ways of intimacy and find greater wholeness. We will soon learn more ways of praying that go beyond the verbal and to the language of the heart where relationships blossom.

Waiting Expectantly at the Edge

The Irish word for *contemplation* means "on the edge of waiting." For the word *edge*, imagine a knife's edge. Notice the kind of expectancy associated with that turn of phrase. If a man in Ireland were to leave his mother and father for the monastic life, that contemplative community would be considered to be *on the edge of waiting*.[2] This is such an intriguing way of appreciating how God uses wordless prayer to continually invite us to more at the edge. More life. More health. More communion. As we wait upon the Lord, God renews our strength from the boundless reserves of God's love.

In Greek, we see something similar is happening with the language around contemplation. Contemplative prayer in Greek is *nipsis* (or *nepsis*) and means "watchfulness." It indicates attentiveness to one's emotions, intentions, and thoughts and remaining in a state of attention to God. We give our focus to God's presence while releasing our selfish and egoistic thoughts. We disregard any other temptations and distractions.

Spiritual formation happens through the practices that engage us more deeply with the essence of the Divine and what nurtures that relationship. Many types and forms of prayer help this along, but fully settling into a posture of stillness, solitude, and silence as an orientation can direct us toward tender affection. Draw near to the still waters with the Shepherd within your inner landscape so you can drink and be satisfied. The desert elders embodied contemplative spiritual lives like this each day.

Often in Western Christianity, we tend to define prayer in terms of certain communication. We may primarily use language toward God in the form of petitions, intercessions, thanksgiving, praise and worship, and praying extemporaneous invocations. Or maybe we use prewritten prayers or psalms. Many of us have been habituated to bring our requests to God and ask for help, but not as many of us have been encouraged to make sure the conversation and communication are two-sided. It wasn't until I was in my late twenties that I heard that *not* talking during prayer would be just as valuable to my spiritual growth as talking—and maybe more life-changing! Stopping to listen during conversations with other people helps us learn about them. Stopping to listen during prayer helps us learn more deeply from and of God.

Like it or not, forms of prayer that involve language can become a crutch by which precision or personal problem-solving becomes our focus. Have you ever gotten so used to hearing your own voice that you forgot that Someone Else was listening to it? Sometimes a certain prayer format can actually stop the needed spiritual process of undoing us. Prayer should cultivate the ground of our inner lives and help us discover, learn, and remember deeply. If prayer feels stale, unengaging, formal, or routine, we should give up that prayer style for a time to refresh and enliven our relationship with God. Sometimes we may get locked in the performance of our praying. Or we may get tangled in intruding, repetitive thoughts that interfere with simply crawling into the embrace of God, as a nonverbal child might do. Prayer without words invites us to not rely on ourselves but be found in God's presence. It is a format that invites us to *be* rather than to *do*.

Contemplative Cistercian monk and writer Father Thomas Merton wrote toward this idea, saying that "the deepest level of communication is not communication, but communion. It is wordless. It is beyond words, and it is beyond speech, and it is beyond concept."[3] This is the essence of what he termed "prayer of the heart." Prayer communion will alter the territory of your inner world in many renewing ways as it becomes part of your life.

During contemplative prayer, "the mind becomes absorbed in the awareness of God as a living presence and as the source of being of all creatures and sensible forms," says Evagrius in the *Praktikos*.[4] Father Thomas Keating describes it as the "opening of mind and heart—our whole being—to God, the Ultimate Mystery. [This situates us] beyond thoughts, words, and emotions." Keating adds that "we know by faith that God is within us and is closer than breathing, closer than thinking, closer than choosing, closer than consciousness itself."[5] Through grace from God, we open our awareness to God. Even as we engage in *unknowing* many of the ways we have learned and known how to pray, we can be born anew in spiritual intimacy. Like a wordless infant being held close in the bosom and feeling the loving gaze of the Divine, we can rest quietly—but not passively. We can let grace be ours. These still waters nourish and revive places in our inner landscapes.

First-century Dionysius the Areopagite was a judge in Athens and one of the first Athenians to believe in Jesus from the apostle Paul's discourse at the Areopagus. He later became the first Christian bishop in Athens. Here's a paraphrase of his explanation of how we enter into the mystery of God through quietness and contemplative prayer: "As we move further into contemplation, our purely intelligible expressions become limited. As we move into the unknown Darkness which is beyond the intellect, our speech is not only limited, but can become absolute silence, of images, thoughts, and as well as of words. According to this degree of transcendence, we can ascend so far that we become wholly voiceless, in proportion to the degree we are absorbed in [God] who is totally ineffable."[6]

Contemplative prayer can be seen as a category bucket: a way to know God that contains many types and styles of silent or wordless prayer. Spiritual guides may categorize contemplative prayer in different ways. Now we will look briefly at two specific ways of praying that can lead us into contemplative awareness of and communion with Divine presence. When they become frequent in your life, you find renewal and wholeness over time. They are forms of prayer that orient our cores to God's will and ways.

The Jesus Prayer

The *Philokalia* is a collection of texts written by the desert elders (including Evagrius Ponticus) and many other teachers that spans from the fourth century to the eighteenth century. You may remember from chapter 2 that those in the Eastern Christian tradition who claimed desert monasticism as their lineage emphasized ascetic devotion. The *Philokalia* was gathered to guide monks living this kind of contemplative life, but its teachings have since spread throughout the laity as well. Many of the texts speak to the spiritual method called *hesychasm*, which means "to keep stillness."[7] The hesychasm teachings focus on the ways of life and the practice of inner prayer that pursues union with God—the One who transcends images, concepts, and languages.[8] These include practices of contemplative prayer, quiet sitting, and mindful recitation of what is known as the Jesus Prayer.

The Jesus Prayer has a few different variations, but it is commonly prayed with these words: "Lord, Jesus Christ, Son of God, have mercy on me, a sinner." The words of the Jesus Prayer derive from the parable of the Pharisee and the publican (tax collector), which Jesus shares in Luke 18:9–14: In the temple are two men. The Pharisee—blameless according to the laws of Moses—prays, "God, I thank you that I am not like other people—robbers, evildoers, adulterers—or even like this tax collector. I fast twice a week and give a tenth of all I get."

Jesus zooms the story in on the tax collector. Such a person would have been a corrupt and despised sinner in the minds of the listening crowd. "But the tax collector stood at a distance. He would not even look up to heaven, but beat his breast and said, 'God, have mercy on me, a sinner'" (Luke 18:13). Then Jesus delivers the final shocker, saying, "I tell you that this man, rather than the other, went home justified before God. For all those who exalt themselves will be humbled, and those who humble themselves will be exalted" (Luke 18:14). The Jesus Prayer helps us keep the virtue of humility embedded in the moments of our day, as it helps us set aside self-righteousness.

For Eastern Christians, the hesychast teachings—a focus on a quiet and supple heart—are considered as important as the sacraments and the liturgy of the Orthodox Church. The need for a spiritual guide is emphasized as well. Spiritual teachers of the East encourage the continual praying of the Jesus Prayer for a life of humble devotion.

Throughout Christian history, some mystics and contemplatives were known to have visions, revelations, and experiences of ecstasy through contemplative practices. But the Orthodox tradition warns about seeking out those experiences. These experiences, they advise, should be viewed as possible secondary outcomes as one seeks intimacy with God. Spiritual practices like fasting, prayer, and worship have a main goal: to ready the heart for the ministries of God's grace. As we've been learning time and again, these attitudes and practices loosen the soil of our interior lands into good ground for the divine seeds of God.

Centering Prayer

If we aren't accustomed to sitting in silence or praying without words, we can start with some training wheels. There is a well-regarded practice that helps prepare us called "centering prayer." For this form of prayer, you choose a sacred word that symbolizes your intention to consent to God's presence and action within you. The contemplative author Keating focused much of his life's work on teaching centering prayer and explaining its spiritual and psychological benefits. He said, "As prayer becomes more intimate, grace reaches down into the psyche, empowering it to unload the emotional damage and debris of a lifetime."[9]

During the time of centering prayer, whenever you find yourself distracted by thoughts, feelings, images, bodily sensations, or things around you, you can return your attention ever so gently to the sacred word you selected. Your sacred word could also be a short phrase or a verse from Scripture. What's important is that it symbolizes, for you, your consent to God's presence and action within you. It doesn't need to be endlessly repeated—unless your distracting thoughts go on nonstop, which might be the case sometimes! People who practice this prayer often find that, sooner or later, their distracting thoughts drop away, enabling them to rest in a spacious, silent sense of God's presence. Of course, such graced moments are not assured to us. If, or when, these placid moments do come, they often do not last very long. As you keep silent before God, whenever a distracting thought arises, you simply return to your sacred word and continue to do so until your prayer time ends. Through this simple but steady way of prayer, our hearts are reoriented.

You may have noticed that other religions have contemplative spiritual aspects to them as well. Some forms of Buddhist and Hindu meditation involve the use of a sound or word called a *mantra*. The primary difference between using a mantra and the sacred word of centering prayer is that a mantra typically is repeated continuously during the time of meditation. An organization called the World Community for Christian Meditation (WCCM), founded by Brother John Main, supports a form of Christian meditation that includes the use of a mantra. WCCM advocates using the Aramaic word *maranatha* (meaning "Come, O Lord") for use in prayer. But other words or phrases may also be used—perhaps words like *peace, listen,* or *Jesus.*

Spiritual director Dr. Lerita Coleman Brown mentioned to me during an interview for *Spark My Muse* that she often uses the prayer phrases "Let me remember that I am one with God" and "Peace be still." By keeping the word or phrase meaningful but simple, we can more easily enter into a nonverbal and nonconceptual period in prayer that doesn't hook in on ideas or language but instead allows us to give ourselves over to God and truly consent to God's healing of our core wounds that rely only on grace.

Dealing with Distractions

As you try to give full attention to God in prayer, thoughts will occur that distract you. This is true no matter what form of contemplative prayer you encounter. At first, your mind may feel like it's busy or buzzing with activity, like a hive of bees. It's likely that your brain and body are not used to being disciplined in such a way. Here is how to persist through it:

1. During prayer, when your attention is misled, first try to become aware of that fact. Notice it briefly.

2. Go right back to saying your sacred word or your prayer phrase and bringing your attention to the Divine presence once again.

The act of returning to attention *is* the essence of the practice of the prayer itself. Recentering is centering. The more we are addicted to disruptions, like our phones, screens, games, or emails, the more it will seem, at first, like our brains are rest-less with many incoming thoughts. Yet each interruption is a chance to regain our attention, an opportunity to bring it back to the prayer practice. This super common bouncy-brain phe-nomenon is sometimes lovingly called the "monkey mind." If we try to settle ourselves into silence for even five minutes a few times a day, in a few days we may notice surprising improve-ments. We will likely notice how we can settle down more quickly into a calmer state.

Practices That Heal

As we adapt to the attentive nature of awareness and contempla-tive prayer, something is happening to us physiologically. The longest nerve in the body, called the vagus nerve, is actually being strengthened. This nerve pathway, also called the tenth cranial nerve, is actually a duo that is found on the left and right sides of the body. The vagus nerve starts in the brain stem, travels down the sides of the neck, and then twists throughout the body to each organ and ends in the gut. Stimulation of the vagus nerve achieves what is called higher vagal tone, which is connected to our overall health in terms of reduced inflam-mation, improved immune system response, fewer digestive issues, improved memory, fewer headaches, less depression, and lowered blood pressure. This nerve pathway is respon-sible for the entire parasympathetic nervous system. Thus it helps control the body's response to stress by returning us to a relaxed state after a stressful event. Other ways to stimulate and tone this vital nerve pathway include using our vocal cords (singing, speaking, or humming), getting therapeutic body massages, breathing deeply and slowly, exercising, keeping healthy bacteria in the gut (using living probiotics and avoiding sugar), and splashing cold water on our faces. We should regularly engage in many ways that make our nervous systems strong and healthy.

In the stilled waters of this settled interior silence, we perceive the divine action of God in daily life. We are refreshed by the peeling away—or "unloading," as Keating calls it—of what keeps us stuck. The practice of the Jesus Prayer or centering prayer may reap rewards quickly. You might find that adding this kind of prayer to your life might get off to a great start and may seem to go very well for two or three months, but Keating warns that then it will begin to uncover a much deeper level of discomfort and old pain within. At this point, the first layers of "soul dross" have already been exfoliated, and more challenging healing can begin. Keating recommended that, ideally, we stay with centering prayer for twenty to thirty minutes twice a day. Some people feel spiritually enlivened when the constraints of verbal prayer fall away, and other people never quite find their footing in prayer forms without words or take a liking to them. If you are unfamiliar with silence and stillness in general, give yourself time to adjust.

Because contemplative prayer helps us listen with a hopeful heart and deeply rest in a disposition of trust, something essential softens within us for the divine seeds of God. To this point, author Marc Thomas Shaw wrote in his fascinating book *Dante's Road: The Journey Home for the Modern Soul*, "As I continue to engage in contemplative practices and immerse myself in teachings, I'm more able to see and appreciate each relationship, each wound, each unskillful response along my own journey as part of the process of stripping away the illusion of this all-consuming need. The need for approval and validation was caused by unconscious wounds and fears. Unexamined, these were not vehicles but obstacles to love."[10]

The next chapter contends with what sneaks and peeks, growls and prowls: the prey and predators in the wild land within us. We will look at the wildest and most dangerous places and how to better locate, understand, and even befriend fear. We will also risk what is needed to reveal the vulnerable and unknown self.

Spiritual Practice: Centering Prayer or the Jesus Prayer

Pick one of the two prayer practices introduced in this chapter to encounter for yourself. Refer to those sections of this chapter to guide you.

The Jesus Prayer is often prayed slowly with these words: "Lord, Jesus Christ, Son of God, have mercy on me, a sinner." When I began to use this prayer, I was so troubled by ingrained issues of shame that saying the words "a sinner" generated powerful negative feelings in me of distance from God. Since my spiritual director encouraged me to accept the invitation to encounter the Divine as the loving parent that I longed to have, I decided to replace "a sinner" with "your child." Quite soon, deep from my inner world, I felt a spark of connection instead of shame. Now I use either phrasing and find the prayer to be a grounding practice throughout my day.

Some people use prayer beads as a tactile way to keep track of their prayer practice and stay focused. Each time they complete the whole phrase, they move a bead over to another section. If their mind wanders, they fidget with their beads to relocate themselves and bring their focus back as they move the beads and begin to pray again. Sometimes one clause of the prayer is attached to an inhale, the next to an exhale, and so on to stay in sync with our natural breathing. This brings about a version of what the apostle Paul calls "unceasing prayer."

To try centering prayer, choose a sacred word or short phrase that may have special meaning for you. I often use the words "Thank you" to keep gratitude and *God my Provider* centered in my mind and life. Words like *Jesus*, *Shepherd*, or *peace* have been especially helpful to me as well. But some other word that you cherish may land well with you. You can switch your sacred word each time you pray with the centering prayer form, or you can say the same word and build consistency that you may grow to relish as a devotional practice.

As you pray, remember that the Living God is aware of you and infused in the middle of your inner life during this time of communion.

7

PREDATORS AND PREY

Befriending Our Fears

So far we have examined the climate, weather, and terrain of the wild land within. But if you listen, you can also hear howls, snarls, and squeaks. There are wild animals within us too. The creatures in our interior worlds include both predators and prey: that which is wild and fierce and that which is vulnerable and fearful. As in any ecosystem, each creature has a purpose and helps balance the natural environment. If one kind of creature dominates our interior lives, infestations arise.

In his book *A Hidden Wholeness: The Journey toward an Undivided Life*, Parker J. Palmer describes the soul as a wild animal: "Tough, resilient, savvy, self-sufficient and yet exceedingly shy. If we want to see a wild animal, the last thing we should do is to go crashing through the woods, shouting for the creature to come out. But if we are willing to walk quietly into the woods and sit silently for an hour or two at the base of a tree, the creature we are waiting for may well emerge, and out of the corner of an eye we will catch a glimpse of the precious wildness we seek."[1]

After reading Palmer's words, I began to approach what felt like feral, wary tendencies in myself in quieter and tenderer ways. What if I could stay at the base of a tree in my inner land- scape and wait to see what would emerge? I longed to see if what was wild in me might come out and be better seen and known.

In this chapter, we'll look at two creatures in the animal world that have been called natural enemies: the fox and the rabbit. They are unequal foes, as only one runs from the other in order to not become a meal. One is ferocious, clever, and dangerous; one is completely defenseless. The predator hunts, traps, and kills on instinct. The prey freezes, runs, and hides to survive. Yet in our inner worlds, these animals are not direct adversaries or separate creatures; rather, they represent distinct aspects that exist in us as integrated wholes. In this chapter, the fox and the rabbit will help us explore misunderstood, expelled, or contradictory parts of ourselves.

Both the fox and the rabbit are frequently considered trick- ster characters in lore and myth. The Warner Brothers cartoon characters Wile E. Coyote and Bugs Bunny survive today as entertaining, clownish tricksters in the popular imagination. Many Native American stories and myths feature the archetypal trickster character. In these stories, the trickster is usually male, has magical powers, and is anthropomorphized. The coyote is the most common trickster featured in the Native stories, but other canny animals—such as the rabbit, raven, blue jay, crow, spider, bear, and raccoon—show up too. The trickster crosses boundaries and will often break both physical laws of nature and societal rules. Some trickster-type stories are serious, while others involve humor or reversals of fortune.

Within the stories themselves, the trickster may help out humans or dupe them, usually through surprising ways and plot twists. Sometimes he uses sneaky and upsetting schemes. Though the trickster is clever and outwits others, sometimes he is foolish or greedy and makes terrible mistakes.

Regrettably, the trickster characters used in Native American stories and myths were thoroughly prohibited by Christian missionaries because of their ambiguous and often cunning nature. It seemed to the white European evangelists that the character bore too much resemblance to the devil, so they sought to eradicate this motif.

To me, it seems the trickster meets us head-on in our own moral confusions and emotional quandaries. I believe the trickster archetype can help us appreciate the creative tension and paradox within our internal and lived-out realities. Through this imaginative outlet of personified animal myth, we will now delve into the wildness, complications, and risks of being human. We will also look at the importance of braving the threat of pain in reconciling with the disparate and maybe dangerous parts of ourselves. By befriending the totality of ourselves, our relational bonds can eventually begin to flourish. In this chapter, we'll also look at the healing role of silence and embodied practices in cultivating wholeness.

Untamed Foxes

In Native American folklore and in ancient stories all around the world, the fox serves as a trickster figure. A fox is foxy—wild and clever—but also vulnerable and shy. When I read the book *The Little Prince,* author Antoine de Saint-Exupéry gave me some insights about my inner trickster fox. In this now-classic tale, the little prince has an encounter with a wild fox. Witness now how the wild fox and the little prince long to know each other better in deep friendship:

"Come and play with me," proposed the little prince. "I am so unhappy."

"I cannot play with you," the fox said. "I am not tamed."

"Ah, please excuse me," said the little prince.

But after some thought, he added: "What does that mean—'tame'?"

"You do not live here," said the fox, "what is it you are looking for?"

"I am looking for men," said the little prince. "What does that mean—tame?"

"Men," said the fox. "They have guns and they hunt. It is very disturbing. They also raise chickens. These are their only interests. Are you looking for chickens?"

"No," said the little prince. "I am looking for friends. What does that mean—tame?"

"It is an act too often neglected," said the fox. "It means to establish ties."

"To establish ties?"

"It's just that," said the fox. "To me, you are still nothing more than a little boy who is just like a hundred thousand other little boys. And I have no need of you. And you, on your part, have no need of me. To you, I am nothing more than a fox like a hundred thousand other foxes. But if you tame me, then we shall need each other. To me, you will be unique in all the world. To you, I shall be unique in all the world. . . . Please—tame me!" said the fox.

"I want to very much," the little prince replied. "But I have not much time. I have friends to discover, and a great many things to understand."

"One only understands the things that one tames," said the fox. "Men have no more time to understand anything. They buy things all-ready made at the shops. But there is no shop anywhere where one can buy friendship, and so men have no friends any more. If you want a friend, tame me."[2]

As I read that for the first time, tears streamed down my face. After too many years of feeling divided and wounded, the fox's sentiment was akin to mine. The wild parts of me felt unbefriended. What would it mean to be known to myself—even the ferocious parts? I would have to move toward this familiarity, a kind of taming, before I could offer any meaningful or lasting befriending to others.

This kind of "taming," if you will, doesn't mean forcing ourselves into a domesticated version of something we are not. It means establishing ties with our innermost and largely unknown selves. It is how we come home again to our own embrace and love the spot that is our wild soul so that we may become realigned with the felt sense of Divine Love. It is the place where God makes God's home. In the land of wild things, we are both the little prince and the wild fox. We have estranged parts of ourselves that long for befriending—reintegration. We desire to know the unknown and wild sides of ourselves that we don't understand. It takes time, patience, and settling down to bring these dispersed pieces into communion and concord.

In the story, the fox goes on to explain to the little prince the process of taming—establishing ties. The wild fox warns the little prince that he must be patient as he gets started: "First you will sit down at a little distance from me—like that—in the grass. I shall look at you out of the corner of my eye, and you will say nothing. Words are the source of misunderstandings. But you will sit a little closer to me, every day." Here we see a glimpse of the contemplative world: the one beyond words that can bring healing and wholeness through the intimacy of presence. A true reckoning with ourselves. "You become responsible, forever, for what you have tamed," the wild fox tells the little prince, adding, "Please tame me."[3]

It will feel like a great risk to be vulnerable enough to feel our powerlessness or our wounds and wildness. By validating this—even by just wordlessly glimpsing this place out of the corner of our eyes—we can become better acquainted with our hidden selves. This risk of being fully seen goes against everything we are taught about how to survive in the world at large. In this world—the ego-driven, me-first, take-what-you-can, apex-predator world—we are taught that we must "eat or be eaten." But the wild animal parts of us have soft and vulnerable underbellies too.

Vulnerable Rabbits

While the rabbit—a total vegan, right?—is a far more vulnerable creature than the fox, it often serves as a clever trickster figure in myths and stories. Stories of the rabbit show us the paradoxes of life. These stories show that softness can be strength, treacherous rivals or circumstances can be overcome, and grand reversals of fortune, for good or ill, can be part of our stories too.

We all have trickster bunnies as part of our wild inner landscapes—get used to the idea. The rabbit is a helpless and fragile thing in the wild places. These clever parts of ourselves survive by fleeing and hiding at the first noise or sign of trouble. This is the fearful part of us—the part that senses threat. When things seem precarious or simply unfamiliar, we will, by instinct, go into a defensive mechanism: we'll run. Or perhaps we freeze, trying the "blend-in mode." This rabbit nature is embedded deeply within, but that is nothing to be ashamed of. We must learn about and embrace the naturally frightened rabbit part of us that comes with being human.

From the classic children's book *The Runaway Bunny* by Margaret Wise Brown, I am reminded of how God cares for and loves the trickster rabbit. In the story, a mischievous young bunny conveys to his mother all the imaginative ways he plans to run away from home. Mother Rabbit plays along, but she as the expert trickster. She meets all his brash ideas with her own, and she outmaneuvers him each time. For each of his plans to escape, she tells him the ingenious way that she will find him again with her mother-love. If he turns into a fish that swims away, she will become an angler that catches him; if he becomes a boat that sails off, she will become a gust of wind that guides him; if he becomes a bird that flies high, she will become a tree that he can nest in; and so on.

Like the bunny, we cannot outrun the love of the Divine. Though we may get the urge to flee certain doom or even ambiguity, we cannot run or hide from ourselves, and we cannot run or hide from God—and this is a saving grace.

In the end and through the entire tale, the story told in *The Runaway Bunny* invites me home to the Divine embrace. We turn and return, deeper and more fully, world without end. Though confusing and paradoxical at times, this runaway bunny part of us is not a bug in the system but rather a feature of the system because we have free will to run where we'd like to go. God is aware of our bunny nature and loves us completely. We learn more richly about our existence as we discover for ourselves through experience. The heart—one's core—is God's home, so wherever we go, God is there. We can, over time, learn to remain in the Love, just as Mother Rabbit invites the young bunny to do at the end: "Why don't you just stay here and have a carrot?"

Naming the Fox and the Rabbit

Thoughtful interactions with the predators and prey of our inner lives can create spiritual growth. As you begin to listen to and befriend the foxy fox within, you will notice when the wild side of the fox may become activated. For instance, during a conflict with a family member, you may start to feel feral. As you become aware of the fox within, talk yourself through the moment: "Here is the fox sneaking into this moment to savage

ed—

it. The fox is ready to bite, ready to tear off its share of the meat and take off. I notice you, fox. Things will be OK."

Or if you make a mistake or feel threatened through situations that evoke envy or shame, you may sense the trickster rabbit either dashing away or else freezing in fear and desperately trying to blend in. You may be able to say to this part of you, "There you are, rabbit. You are scared, paralyzed with distress. You are full of worth and needful of grace. Do not be afraid. I receive you. All is well."

The trickster creatures within us instruct us on our emotional bewilderments, complications, and contradictions. Clever and wild. Creative and predatory. Quick and persistent. The fox and rabbit parts of the inner life reside within us on their own terms. Still, we can welcome them both as we notice their paw prints on our inner terrains and gain understanding. We can realize that we are not taming the wildness away; rather, we are integrating the wild parts and befriending the whole of us as we learn more. We protect and validate what is there through receiving, valuing, and nurturing. Remember to deeply appreciate what you can about the qualities of your inner self. Notice the qualities when you see them in your thoughts or when they affect your relationships. Keep notes. Continue to learn from the creatures of the wild and shadowed places.

You may wonder, Can these two creatures really coexist within me? We see this ideal and coinciding paradox featured in the Bible. The imagery of the "lion lying next to the lamb" foreshadows a time of abiding peace and shalom: predator and prey together, and no harm done. I wonder if this isn't only about the external world of nations and empires. I think it can begin within the inner wild land of each person. As you befriend your creatures within, a wholeness of your humanity and a more balanced relationship of the disparate parts of yourself begin. May your fox and your rabbit become your companions. A new world is possible.

Sitting in the Silent Forest

To better know the predators and prey of our wild lands within, we are advised to sit down quietly in the landscape of our inner worlds and wait for the wild things to come out. Wait for them to emerge and be more fully known, as Palmer tells us. If you haven't spent much time in this type of activity, you might be afraid of what sort of wild things will emerge from the unknown. Could the wild creatures arrive and be much scarier than a fox or a rabbit? What if something hidden is so monstrous that when you look at it, all you see are sharp teeth and it tries to eat you alive?

So it's time to talk about fear. When we aren't very acquainted with inner silence, silence can be awkward, disconcerting, and frightening. For some, it seems like this sort of soul silence might yawn into an abyss, giving us entry into a place of total unknown and unwelcome. Ask yourself honestly, How comfortable am I with silence?

Silence can carry negative meanings for us. Maybe we've been given the "silent treatment." Maybe we've been silenced by others who were dominant and now we need to express ourselves. And think about what happens when we get silence from God. When we ask God for something and we only hear silence in reply, we may find ourselves in a state of chaos, disappointment, or confusion. Why is God silent? we may wonder. How should we understand silence when God does it?

At first, we might think of silence as God's answer of no to a prayer request. Instead, we should listen more deeply. Silence is its own unique answer. Contemplative author Carl McColman and cohost of the *Embracing Silence* podcast suggests that silence can teach us about ourselves.[4] We can find comfort in silence as we understand it to be God's presence because silence is a language of God. It may not convey the answer we desire, but it is an answer we can learn from. We are wise to perceive it in the fullness of its own matchless language.

Certainly silence can be eerie or uncomfortable. Within the long stints of silence at nighttime, we may hear strange and creepy "bumps in the night." It is in the quiet that feelings of dread, doubt, or disappointment can emerge too. In silence, we must reconcile with ourselves. The veneer of our defenses will fail us at some point, and we will come into contact with our loneliness. Henri Nouwen writes, "To live a spiritual life we must first find the courage to enter into the desert of our loneliness and to change it by gentle and persistent efforts into a garden of solitude. The movement from loneliness to solitude, however, is the beginning of any spiritual life because it is the movement from the restless senses to the restful spirit, from the outward-reaching cravings to the inward-reaching search, from the fearful clinging to the fearless play."[5]

Many of us would rather be distracted, occupied, and busy rather than settle into an extended time of quietness or stillness in the wilderness of our wild lands. Maybe we don't have the patience or the stomach to wait quietly and see what comes out. For some of us, it's too disturbing. Unpleasant thoughts arise during long stretches of noiselessness. At times, the hush might feel downright hellish.

Undoubtedly, interior quiet spaces create the time for reconciling unsettled business. Trauma can surface. Bitterness can rise. Old wounds can reopen. Conflict within skulks like monsters looking for prey. We may curate our lives so we do not endure periods of silence for too long. Yet inner silence is a potential place of wholeness. Silence, in the form of peace *from* mind, comes through the Divine Spirit so we can be made new—not by trying anything but by releasing everything.

In the process of making space for silence for your interior world, do not be surprised if—or rather, *when*—you have a rough start. Restlessness, anger, guilt, anxiety, regret, jealousy, shame, trauma, boredom, betrayals, old wounds: these and all sorts of other issues can find their way to the surface of our consciousness and vie for our attention when we begin making space for silence and stillness. Our minds might start to race with it all. Anything you haven't healed from properly or anything you haven't sorted through with the help of God (and sometimes a trained therapist) can howl or pounce. It takes true courage to enter the silent wild places alone without the idols or fig leaves we keep with us to make us more comfortable or help us feel empowered.

If you fear the wilderness of silence, you have a perfectly good reason to. Even Jesus was bedeviled there. When fear or discomfort confronts us in our first experiences with genuine interior silence, we must remember that we are in good company. What we are experiencing is normal. When it gets tedious or the ghosts of past presences begin to haunt us like predators, we might see it as a sign to flee. Stay put: wait for the silence and stillness to teach you something.

As deeply as we try to bury or forget our inner selves, some wiser part of us—that deep kernel—will try to reintegrate us into shalom with Spirit. The Spirit of Love is an unstoppable force that heals and makes whole all that is disconnected. And the Divine calls to us, irresistibly, *from* the deep and unknown places. If silence feels too scary, start small, but keep sitting with it and building your courage.

Notice the Fear You Avoid

What if you feel like a castaway on a shadowy island of fear with only your torments for company? Let's look at things we can do with our fears and take an inventory to gain key understandings of them.

First, noticing that we have a fear of what we will find in silence and solitude is a positive initial step. Many people do not even get to this first step. Some of us simply believe—for a long time—that something *else* is going on: "Oh, it's not fear. I'm just an introvert" or "I'm not afraid; I'm just a busy person. Too much to do right now to get to the bottom of this. Maybe when things calm down."

When we are fearful, we may have anxious habits, compulsive behaviors, chronic frustrations, insecurity issues, procrastination patterns, and interpersonal problems. We may micromanage; often feel stressed out; overconsume; have compulsive thoughts or behaviors; often need validation;

have sleeping problems, headaches, or stomach problems; or feel jealousy. As fearful people, we may experience disordered habits of eating, the need for distractions, the consuming need to voice our opinions or find affirmation, ongoing perfectionism, and binging behavior. All these point to difficulties with fear and trying to avoid fear.

If you have any of these issues, congratulations! You are a typical human being. Fear is normal. It helps us stay alive. The human species would have gone extinct without the type of fear that prompts us into actions for basic survival. Fear enables the rabbit creature of your inner world to run and hide when you are facing true emotional or spiritual danger. Fear is what prompts the wild fox predator within to use clever tricks to outwit and get a meal.

We all try to deal with fear in various ways, both healthy and unhealthy. Let's always remember, however, that *avoiding* the fear that arises—especially the kind that arises in silence or solitude—is terrible hygiene for the soul. It makes the creatures of our inner worlds become filthy, rabid beasts, infesting and even terrorizing many areas of our inner landscapes.

Watch Your Fear Happen

Even though we may experience fear very powerfully, we can remember that we are *not* our fears. Remember our teacher Evagrius? As humans, we are quite susceptible to overidentifying with our fearful thoughts and feelings. We tend to attach to the burden of enormous shame and embarrassment about our thoughts, feelings, and fears. I might think of myself as "an afraid person" instead of thinking of myself as a person experiencing fearful thoughts. See the difference? How do you think about yourself?

Let us remember that emotions, such as fear, also blow in like weather. The hissing and snarling you heard in the silence was not a hideous creature; it was bad weather. This weather moves into our inner landscapes and back out again. You can learn to notice and to watch your fear happen.

There tend to only be a few main kinds of fear, so get to know how they move in the wild places. Some are psychosocial, such as being frightened of ridicule, embarrassment, humiliation, or shame. Any level of worry or phobia regarding failure or rejection fits in this category too. Fears of impotence include a frightened sense of powerlessness and loss; pain or harm; and abandonment, being alone, or being unsafe. And the existential dread of death counts too—hardwired into the species, that one!

John O'Donohue gives us sage advice: "When you cease to fear your solitude, a new creativity awakens in you. Your forgotten or neglected wealth begins to reveal itself. You come home to yourself and learn to rest within. Thoughts are our inner senses. Infused with silence and solitude, they bring out the mystery of inner landscape."[6] The soul hears best in the Divine silence. It is the place of the presence of God. Out of the silence, God whispers to the soul, "Come and be embraced." Here we find that we are known and the fullness of all things is glimpsed. When attuned, one hears with the whole self and is transfigured.

Be Curious about Your Fear

A true shift in our personal perceptions about fear makes all the difference. Fear does not have to be feared because it has useful purposes. Can we have some curiosity about it? I think that we can also live better with natural occurrences of fear if we understand the important reason that we have fear in the first place. Fear is part of our biological warning systems; it serves us like a car's dashboard serves us, with dials or screens.

The dashboard screen is not what makes the car go; the motor does. The screen or dials can help us understand what is happening inside the workings of the car and give us helpful information. Sometimes a vehicle sensor goes bad and we need to replace it and reset the system so that the dashboard doesn't light up like a tacky Christmas tree. Our bodies give us feedback when we stop good habits of self-care. You may start to feel really upset and exhausted and maybe even ill—and then you realize, "Wait. I'm getting signals! I think I'm overdoing it, and I'd better make some changes. Naptime!"

When an internal area needs attention, it is fear that helps us know this. If we haven't practiced being quiet and listening properly, we won't grasp that sense of fear for what it is. Instead, fear will often show up as a neurotic or controlling behavior. When we haven't given ourselves the proper space, time, and ways to heal, we mindlessly resort to neurotic ways to deflect our suffering.

Donna was a woman who used to get up at night and check the locks on all her doors and windows. She checked them before she went to bed too, but because of habits of fear, if she heard a sound at night, she'd get up and double- or triple-check.

By asking herself questions based in curiosity, Donna realized a lot about her fearful behavior and feelings. The chance of a break-in was near zero, but when Donna felt extra anxious in life, this habit would show up in bigger ways. It's something her mother started doing after an incident with an angry boyfriend. Because she also felt shame about her fear, Donna felt locked in place emotionally. Once she felt safe again in her body and investigated her habits and deeper issues of worry, she could better understand that her fear surfaced as neurotic safety checks.

I have good news: on the other side of fear is relief. In fact, instead of being in combat mode against our fears—fighting them, defending ourselves against them, and battling them to the death—we can try something we rarely consider. We can strike a posture of curiosity toward it, like Donna did. Being curious about our fears is an investigative way to move forward without judgment. Like a detective, we can scan our inner worlds for clues and more information. It can be very empowering. When we are curious, our brains shift away from panic into a very different mode—one of flexibility and engagement. This is the vantage point where insights are sparked and growth is not just possible but likely.

Converse with Your Fear

We don't have to hunt fear with a pitchfork. Fear has something to say. Our fears offer us an invitation to engage with the discomfort of the inner places. Will you give your fear a chance to speak to you?

When you realize that you are afraid or not doing well, sit down with your fear and have a conversation. Here are three ways to converse with fear: First, when you feel or notice discomfort, pause. Stay paused until you know more. Second, acknowledge what is happening in the moment. Be honest: "This feels bad—negative. What do I feel? Maybe it is fear, but I'm also angry. What else? I feel overlooked." Third, dig a bit deeper. Ask, What is this trying to show me? or What else might be going on? Give yourself some time, and delve into the fear: "I'm not sure why I'm angry. Now, thinking about it more, it wasn't such a good day. Three things happened today that made me feel frustrated, inferior, and like I wasn't being taken seriously."

As you take up a conversation with your fear, remember this: sidestep the shame. Shame will tell you horrible things about yourself. But when we are curious about our fears, we can allow the shame to move along downstream without its debris attaching to us.

Embarrassment or shame will likely put us in a rabbit freeze-or-runaway mode. Denial, anger, and deflection are other unhelpful responses. Instead, let's encounter the fear or the discomfort with some questions and curiosity. And then, once we've noticed something new, we move on.

The self-dialogue can go something like this: "Why do I always swing out of control? I'm such an idiot. No, wait. . . . I'm not going to also spin into a shame whirlpool. A lot of people get frustrated over or afraid of the same types of things. I don't have to beat myself up. These feelings will eventually pass, just like a storm passes or the water goes downstream."

Befriend Your Fear

As strange as it may sound, once you get to the point of regularly dialoguing with your fears, you may now be ready to approach your fear as a friend. You've noticed it, watched it, and been curious about it, and you've conversed with it. Curiosity and generosity build connections, even with and within yourself. As humans, we are relational beings by design. We even relate to *ourselves* in connective ways that build trust with ourselves. Kindness—even to ourselves—matters.

This idea of befriending your fear might come as a surprise, but it will serve you well. Along with everything else, always give yourself a chance to play, move, or feel safe—bodily—as you *process* fear. We can't *think* our way out of being fearful. But we can use tactics that allow us to reengage the parts of our brains with our body sensations that have gone offline during a fear response and still need to be processed.

A path forward can look like this: Step back to reflect and disengage from the potency of the fearful situation. Feel yourself back into the physicality of your body, maybe through a walk, some exercises, or some slow breathing. Give yourself the time you need. Once you are ready, you can ask yourself a few nonthreatening questions to think more coherently. These three can help: What am I actually concerned about? What am I afraid will happen? and What is the worst thing that could happen in this moment?

When you ask questions of yourself—just like when you speak with a friend—you may get more questions from asking questions than you get answers. You can hold those questions for a while and let them chill to room temperature. Sometimes, at first, they are simply too hot to handle or too cold to hold. Once you are in a neutral place with your fear, you may be able to identify characteristics of it you were not able to see before. Wait in silence or stillness to see what else emerges. In the space of interior silence, when we finally get underneath our neurotic behaviors that work to camouflage our fears, we can discover what is freezing and blocking us. Take note of what it is. See if you notice patterns over time.

Once you make time and space for silence, move past the decoys of distraction and busyness to your core fears. Then give yourself the opportunity to observe and be curious about your fear. Converse with it, and you may find that you are even able to befriend it. After all, Jesus says love your enemies.

In the next chapter, we will get into the hardest territory of the inner world: the places of grief, loss, bereavement, suffering, and trauma. These are territories common to every human. The pain is also held collectively and interconnectedly in subterranean places within, sorted by groups. Instead of avoiding these areas, we will learn of them and traverse through them.

Spiritual Practice: *Lectio Divina*

Lectio Divina means "sacred reading." It is an age-old reading and prayer devotional practice that has four elements. First, we read and listen carefully to a short passage of Scripture. Second, we reflect and meditate on its meaning. Third, we respond to what we've meditated on through mental or verbal prayer. And last, we rest in a prayerfully receptive state while being aware of the presence of God. This practice helps us cultivate a deep inner attention to the Divine presence communicated through Scripture. The process of Lectio Divina can be communicated in shorthand today as *read, reflect, respond, rest.*

Here is a guide to the practice of Lectio Divina. Select one of the verses listed next or one of your favorites, and work through the four movements of this practice.

1. *Read.* Select a verse to read slowly and with care at least three times through. Reading it aloud can be extra helpful. Give yourself time to absorb the richness of the text.

2. *Reflect.* Dwell on a word or segment of the reading that catches your attention. Consider what this can speak into your life, and hold space to meditate on it. Allow the Spirit to teach you. Roll the words over in your understanding for a few moments.

3. *Respond.* Take your meditative thoughts or questions to God in prayer. Ask for guidance and God's presence to be with you as you receive this passage in a deeper way in your life and inner world. As you continue to pray, begin to include pauses and places of silence.

4. *Rest.* Allow the places of silence to enlarge and then envelop your words of prayer so that your prayer becomes a posture of silent rest, listening, and being aware that God's presence is with you. Stay with this time of silence for several minutes, or as long as you are able, to cultivate restoration for your soul.

Verse Selections:

Psalm 27:1: The Lord is my light and my salvation—whom shall I fear? The Lord is the stronghold of my life—of whom shall I be afraid?

Psalm 56:3–4: When I am afraid, I put my trust in you. In God, whose word I praise—in God I trust and am not afraid. What can mere mortals do to me?

Psalm 59:16: But I will sing of your strength, in the morning I will sing of your love; for you are my fortress, my refuge in times of trouble.

1 John 4:18–19: There is no fear in love. But perfect love drives out fear, because fear has to do with punishment. The one who fears is not made perfect in love. We love because he first loved us.

8

FIRE BOGS

Trekking through Trauma and Loss

In 1921, city officials of Tulsa, Oklahoma, conspired with white citizens to attack Black residents and their businesses in the thriving Greenwood District. In what became known as the Tulsa Race Massacre, the coordinated bloodshed and destruction dealt a terrible blow to the heart of the most prosperous freedom colony established by emancipated slaves in the segregated South.

The situation began near the courthouse when a crowd of white men gathered after the arrest of a young Black man, Dick Rowland, accused of sexually assaulting a young white woman, Sarah Page. Once rumors of a lynching spread to Greenwood, some fifty to seventy Black residents came armed to the courthouse to ensure justice and security for Mr. Rowland. A white man threatened to take a rifle from a Black man who was a recently returned veteran of World War I. An argument ensued, and shots were fired. Ten white men and two Black men were killed.

News of the incident raged through the city, and violence soon erupted. Then came an organized and deadly string of days-long retaliative terror to the Black residents of Greenwood. The Tulsa police deputized furious white men from the failed lynching mob and encouraged them to shoot Black people dead. Hundreds of white Tulsa residents raided the Black district. They looted and fired rounds of bullets at families and business owners. The Black residents fired back, hoping to defend their lives and their properties. The police supported the white rioters by arresting Black people involved in skirmishes. City officials and police allowed various kinds of planned violence to go unimpeded, and sometimes they joined in the destruction themselves.

The next day was far worse. Thousands of enraged white people arrived and descended on Greenwood. They shot, burned, looted, and bombed the area until more than thirty-five square blocks of the wealthiest Black community in the United States were devastated, leaving about ten thousand Black people homeless. From overhead aircraft, the Tulsa National Guard shot at Black residents as they ran for cover.[1]

The most flourishing district that Black people had created for themselves following the American chattel slavery era came to ruin—in all, 1,256 houses by arson, several churches, a junior high school, 191 businesses, and the only hospital in the district available to care for Black people under the segregation laws of Oklahoma. Many hundreds of Black residents were wounded, up to three hundred were killed, and more than six thousand homeless were interned at facilities.

In the end, not one white person was convicted of charges for any injuries, deaths, or property damage, which came to an adjusted $32 million in 2019.[2] In the eventual trial for the accused young man, Mr. Rowland, it became clear that what actually transpired was innocuous. Whether he tripped and steadied himself by grabbing her arm or stepped on her foot as he exited the elevator that Miss Page was operating, she let out a yelp in surprise. Upon seeing Mr. Rowland leave the building quickly and thinking Miss Page looked distressed, a nearby clerk assumed she had been attacked. The white man panicked and immediately sought the authorities for Mr. Rowland's arrest for sexual assault before knowing information about what occurred. After he was arrested, a white lynch mob assembled quickly to kill him. Never did Miss Page express an interest in pressing charges, and subsequent investigations found that no harm had been done.

Many Black people relocated from Greenwood, and the ones who stayed almost never spoke about those days of destruction and murder. Though the occurrence initially made national news, in the ensuing years, the incident became a taboo subject for many. Officials had it omitted from local and state history books. The trauma, grief, and loss within the Black community during and after the Tulsa Race Massacre were immeasurable, and they encompass several categories of loss we will learn about in this chapter. These types of losses result in intense sorrow and anguish that can last generations. We will now explore the most difficult terrain of the inner landscape, which I call *fire bogs*.

Trauma occurs when a person becomes mentally and emotionally overwhelmed from experiencing too much, experiencing something too soon, or experiencing something too fast.[3]

Loss and suffering happen on various levels. It may be related to our age (such as exposure to violence or sexual material as a child), to a quick or compounding succession of harms (such as experiencing several losses of loved ones during a short time period), or to the depth and impacts of the change that created losses (a severe accident, divorce, or sudden relocation). Grief disrupts the continuity of meaning in our lives. Large griefs, small griefs—they all count. They all create fire bogs in our wild lands within.

In this chapter, we will look at collective trauma and a spirituality sturdy enough to sustain people in dire times. We will also look at grief and loss of a personal but indefinite nature, such as the decline and death of a loved one, as well as the doubts that come from loss and suffering that may injure or dismantle our faith.

Not just catastrophic loss, like death or destruction, can create terrible grief. The loss can be the loss of a dream, our innocence, a home, a job, a relationship, a way of life, or an expectation to which we've been attached. A collapse of our faith, a discarding of the religion or perspective within which we grew up, or a period of spiritual deconstruction—these are themselves losses as well that need to be grieved.

It can be enticing to try to look the other way or to skirt the fire bogs of our inner worlds. But we must venture *through* these places of suffering to find wholeness. Though many of us wish to avoid these hard places or pretend they don't exist, ignoring them often reaps consequences of deeper pain.

Trauma changes us. The brain's chemistry is intimately involved in trauma. Dr. Bessel A. van der Kolk explains that when we experience trauma, the brain works to protect us. It literally creates a new personality on top of the one we were born with and transforms us. The flight, fight, and freeze part of the brain goes into overdrive, the hypothalamus gets stuck in hyperdrive, and the prefrontal cortex becomes neglected and undeveloped. This makes us less able to learn by constantly injecting stress hormones into the bloodstream.[4]

No one's terrain of suffering and trauma can be compared to someone else's. Any fire bog is a place of personal turmoil, one that others cannot even pretend to understand. Of suffering, John O'Donohue writes, "There is the solitude of suffering, when you go through darkness that is lonely, intense, and terrible. Words become powerless to express your pain; what others hear from your words is so distant and different from what you are actually suffering."[5]

Communal Trauma

Experiencing speechless terror and the unspeakable that creates lasting scars can happen to us as individuals but also to entire communities and groups. Those eighteen hours of the Tulsa Race Massacre were a microcosm of the larger Black experience in the United States. Between the years 1880 and 1940, nearly five thousand Black men, women, and children were lynched. Ordinarily, lynching happened when a group of white people would capture and murder a Black person or Black persons, usually by hanging and often in public, for alleged offenses. Many times Black people were killed as a form of ongoing terror and to force social and political subordination to whites. These were efforts to enforce claims of supremacy and create lessons and reminders of inferiority to the people group they despised. Those murdered were stripped of their human and legal rights, as they had no opportunities for trials if or when they were accused of a crime. Rarely was anyone held culpable for taking part in these murders and their related criminality—sometimes whole towns gathered for the spectacle that would be announced in the local paper. Black bodies were often beaten, mutilated, and burned, and an entire industry of selling postcard photographs emerged that commemorated public lynching deaths. By the thousands, graphically grue-some cards were purchased by white onlookers to be mailed across the nation with salutations and the latest lynching news. Authorities in counties, police departments, and government looked the other way while it happened—regularly allowing white vigilante mobs to take Black prisoners from their jail cells or custody to be publicly executed before a jeering mob before court trials could occur.

Dr. James H. Cone notes the striking similarity between the humiliating public execution of Jesus on a Roman cross and the lawless lynching of thousands of Black people strung up to die on trees. If we commonly called the miscarriage of justice and wrongful execution of Jesus a lynching instead of a cruci-fixion, would we still theologize it into a theory of atonement? Cone potently reveals how the suffering on the cross and the lynching tree interpret each other. "Both were public spectacles, shameful events, instruments of punishment reserved for the most despised people in society," he writes. "Any genuine theol-ogy and any genuine preaching of the Christian gospel must be measured against the test of the scandal of the cross and the lynching tree."[6]

The trauma that occurs against systematically and historically mistreated groups creates certain features of wounded landscapes in the interior lives not only of individuals but also of whole communities and in the perpetrators as well. Reconciling and restoring people of different histories and colors involves first realizing the immense harm that trauma has had and still has in the lives of Black, Indigenous, Latinx, and people of color (BILPOC). As we move to be whole and integrated within ourselves and with God, we must take into consideration how different the trauma landscape may be for different people according to how violence has occurred in their family and community histories.

Types of Loss

When typical categories fail to hold a space for our pain, we suffer what is called *ambiguous loss*, or grief. This covers many areas of lived experiences. There are some occasions we don't consider as often, such as caring for a debilitated parent, experiencing chronic illness or addiction issues, going through a divorce, relocating, and others. Worse yet, other people may not know how to help us; they may minimize our pain or evade it. Ambiguous loss is something all of us experience in some form, and dealing with it might feel like getting stuck or slogging through in a sticky bog of everlasting fire.

When our grief is unnoticed or when we grieve a loss that is misunderstood, goes unrecognized, or is unaccompanied, that grief becomes *disenfranchised*. This means that within society, some losses are recognized and engaged with for healing;

other losses that are just as painful to endure are not noticed or treated as equally legitimate. They can be invisible in public, and during our grieving, we feel more alone or somehow illegitimate as we suffer.

A few examples of disenfranchised grief include the following:

- vicarious trauma
- systematic oppression, like sexism, racism, and prejudice
- forms of rejection and isolation
- domestic abuse and societal violence
- not being able to become a parent
- a prolonged crisis or illness
- an ongoing physical or mental difficulty
- caring for a child with special needs or an aging family member

Many people closely associate grief with death, but grief is actually a more basic and a more commonly occurring human emotion that expands beyond issues of death. We will experience a sense of grief as we become aware of and distressed because of a loss. Here are six types of loss that can arise in our lives.

Loss of relationship. This could include the loss of a friend, family member, or significant other through any circumstance: breakup, separation, divorce, illness, or death.

Loss of a role. This loss occurs when we lose an identity we once had. It includes things such as job loss, demotion, change of occupation or vocation, or retirement; the death of a child; the era in which one's children leave home; and the loss of someone or something one was attached to or responsible to care for, including a pet.

A functional loss. A functional loss is one of being physically unable to do something, get somewhere, or continue at the same level of aptitude, skill, or memory.

Material loss. This loss is that of physical objects, like possessions, shelter, money, transportation, access to food, and clothing.

Intrapsychic loss. This involves mental and emotional phenomena. It may refer to wishes, thoughts, impulses, and expectations in the mind. When we've had dreams deferred or plans squashed, those losses fit into this category as well.

Systemic loss. This kind of loss encompasses more than the individual or a few people. It involves the change or the breakdown of important stabilizing societal factors at a national or even global scale. Tremendous systemic losses include those experienced during or due to a pandemic, famine, genocide, war, racism, sustained civil unrest, and so on. The worldwide response to the COVID-19 pandemic has irrevocably changed our interactions, friendships, communications, life experiences, travels, jobs, ways of worship, and much more. It is no surprise that mental distress, intense displays of emotion and behavior, and difficulties coping seem to be widespread.

The Forever Bog

The worst fire bog of my inner landscape felt like a decade-long siege of my soul. It started two weeks before winter break during my sophomore year of college when I got a phone call in my dorm room. My father had been admitted to the intensive care unit, having had a stroke in his brain stem, and I was told to come right away. He was only forty-four years old.

Somehow, my father survived the stroke, but he was incapacitated and sustained severe brain damage. He could never move or speak again. So during the entire decade of my twenties, my father was locked in somewhere between life and death, languishing in a few different nursing homes for the rest of his life. The doctors fitted a feeding tube in his stomach and attached ventilator tubes to a tracheotomy hole they had cut into his neck to help with his breathing. There he remained, day after day, usually in a wakeful unconscious state. His eyes might be open, but they didn't track anything anymore. I could not really say goodbye to him because he still lived. Yet he was absent from my life in all the ways I deeply wanted to and had been able to connect to him.

The loss was utterly gut-wrenching and perpetual. Overwhelming sorrow flooded me during each visit, and this era of grief ran on a loop. Sometimes the anguish collected into a kind of stone within, which made it feel too painful to even visit him. But since he was occasionally responsive to my questions, by blinking twice for yes and once for no, I had consuming guilt that he might be missing me when I didn't make trips to see him. It seemed no one understood this type of bottomless, repeated torment that went on unabated, year after year after year.

In my particular situation, it felt like nothing soothed the fire that ravaged in the bog within. It was typical grief, plus ambiguous loss and disenfranchised grief. Additionally, the previous and ongoing trauma in my family felt impossible to resolve. My parents' fraught relationship and eventual divorce had been full of pain and tumult, and it was hard for me to find much sense of equilibrium during these times. These factors had shaped my childhood and my adolescence. Now as a college student and young adult, I was in continual soul-battering mourning, which further disoriented me and took me into a desert of darkness and desolation. On this front, nothing made sense.

My circumstance seemed so complicated and awkward to describe—and clearly not a fitting conversation choice at parties. When kind folks offered consolation, it usually fell short of my need. For people who tried to stay abreast of the matter or tried to be helpful, their words got predictable. "How's your dad?" they would ask, month after month and then year after year.

"He's the same. He's probably always going to be the same," I'd say.

Then maybe there would be an awkward pause. "I hope he gets better. I'll pray that God heals him," they might reply.

My confusion and diet of ongoing trauma deeply affected all my relationships. No part of my family wasn't somehow marred by the bizarre tragedy. In its wake, a host of morbid and stranger things occurred too. At one point, someone told me, "Insurance agents are using your dad's story to sell life and disability insurance."

I felt my stomach drop. "Wait. What?" I asked, bewildered.

"Yeah. Probably because he was so young and healthy, and it came out of nowhere," the person continued. "You just never know," they said.

Though insurance agents were profiting from my young father's story, my family was stressed and splintering. My pain didn't subside. In many ways, God became more perplexing and unfathomable. The God I was taught about as a child—the one who answers yes to faithful prayer warriors—fell to the ground in pieces and shattered like a deaf idol of sandstone.

Suffering and Spirituality

The bogs of grief and trauma and loss have no simple answers. Sometimes the searing pain lasts and lasts. Van der Kolk writes, "Long after a traumatic experience is over, it may be reactivated at the slightest hint of danger and mobilize disturbed brain circuits and secrete massive amounts of stress hormones. This precipitates unpleasant emotions, intense physical sensations, and impulsive and aggressive actions. These post-traumatic reactions feel incomprehensible and overwhelming. Feeling out of control, survivors of trauma often begin to fear that they are damaged to the core and beyond redemption."[7]

During my father's ordeal, I found myself, as van der Kolk describes, often commandeered by stress hormones and anxiety. As most people forgot about the ongoing trauma I was experiencing within, my overreactions or trauma-fueled responses might be deemed as character flaws or as unspiritual ways of grieving. I don't think most people—even my spouse or my best friends—realized then that I was simply in survival mode for such a long time. Decades.

The Conversation and the Community

Writer Annie Dillard speaks to these complex places of suffering. "In the deeps are the violence and terror of which psychology has warned us," she writes. "But if you ride these monsters down, if you drop with them farther over the world's rim, you find what our sciences cannot locate or name, the substrate, the ocean or matrix or ether which buoys the rest, which gives goodness its power for good, and evil its power for evil, the unified field: our complex and inexplicable caring for each other, and for our life together here. This is given. It is not learned."[8]

For healing and restoration to occur, our pain and fears related to loss require periods of bereavement and lament. Bereavement is the condition of being aware of loss through deprivation. Lament is any expression of that bereavement. We need to hold space for these ways to heal as long as we feel the need to experience them.

The Scriptures are full of lament. If you count them up, 61 of the 150 Psalms are entirely ones of lament. Job laments his dreadful condition and cries out in complaint and misery to God. Jesus is recorded as weeping in lament at Lazarus's grave and over the city of Jerusalem and the children of Israel more specifically.

If lament is communal—shared *by* and *within* a community—the painful process through a fire bog becomes less gruesome and taxing. When the repercussions of the loss are given a chance for mitigation, the emotional burden is shouldered by more people. Through communal lament, we experience something like a blanket of support during a bereavement period of suffering.

Expressions of communal bereavement may take the form of rituals: private and public ways of mourning. These may include embodied practices: songs such as requiems and dirges, rituals, and weeping, to name a few. In some places in China, India, and Egypt, crying is so vital to the customs of collective bereavement that professional mourners may be hired.

Sitting shiva is an ancient Jewish seven-day stay-at-home mourning ritual that happens after the death of a family member and is still commonly practiced. It takes into account the need to process grief by slowing down to allow one's emotions to catch up to the reality of the loss and change.[9] During this period, the mourners are cared for by others. Extended family and friends visit to offer condolences to and support the bereaved. Compared to our modern, fast-paced ways of coping with death, shiva allows for plenty of time to process the shock and loss and to find ways to express sorrow. As we process the shock and loss, we can consider our connections to our departed loved ones with others, and we can slowly reenter society feeling a little more grounded and prepared.

In the United States, there is often pressure to move quickly through the grieving process and to get back to "normal" in just a few days, weeks, or months. But feelings of loss normally extend a long time. The pace of grief is a personal one. Only you can make decisions about it and create boundaries for it. You are allowed to grieve in the way that makes your healing whole. Making peace with our discomfort means that we approach it again and again until we acclimate. Eventually, we recognize ourselves again as having passed through it. Our perspectives shift over time and usually through a gradual process of renewal and acceptance. Allowing lament to be a normal part of life and inviting others into a stage of lament when they are suffering is so vital for spiritual health.

"If grace is so wonderful, why do we have such difficulty recognizing and accepting it?" writes author Kathleen Norris. "Maybe it's because grace is not gentle or made-to-order. It often comes disguised as loss, or failure, or unwelcome change."[10] Grace is the only answer. Grace is senseless too—but beautifully so when we need rescue.

During my father's long suffering, some specific questions began to take shape for me. Is the God who I was taught to believe in someone who can be trusted? In what ways? What is my suffering going to do to my relationship with that God? What does that relationship look like now that the same answers don't work? Can my understanding of who God is and what is happening expand to encompass mystery? Since my expectations of God have been shattered, where can I explore the unfolding questions? What might give me a bigger picture that I can't possibly see from here?

"How can one believe in God in the face of such horrendous suffering as slavery, segregation, and the lynching tree?" writes Cone. "Under these circumstances, doubt is not a denial but an *integral* part of faith. It keeps faith from being sure of itself. But doubt does not have the final word. The final word is faith giving rise to hope."[11]

Indeed, as we move through the doubts and suffering with whatever faith we have and the grace God gives us, we can come out on the other side in one of two ways. We can emerge from the fire bog in disillusionment, bitterness, and unfaithfulness.

Or we can emerge from it with a hope and confidence stronger than before. We can be sustained through fidelity to the sacred unseen. Hope doesn't cure pain, but it builds our courage to keep going.

Many who have experienced deep grief and loss find kinship and guidance in other people who have suffered greatly. To me, Black theologians and spiritual guides offer me hope aplenty. Here is a treasury of wisdom for anyone who will listen on how to endure the hardest excruciations of life and carry on. When I'm deep in sorrow now, I sometimes close my eyes, and in my sacred imagination, I hold the hands of the dear saints. Sometimes I sing along with the spirituals and the liberation songs, and I give my worries back to God. I let the tears flow. In low times, I put on Mahalia Jackson's "How I Got Over" and turn it up loud. I let myself weep and feel the sorrow and realize just how very hard it was. I notice too that yes, I'm still here, and "my soul look back and wonder / how I made it over?"

Spiritual Preparation

If you practice something before you need it, it could save your life during an emergency. When life goes off course in spectacular fashion, drawing on our experiences with a spiritual formation practice will put us in a better position to endure. It's important to be acquainted with and habituated to sustaining spiritual practices *before* tragedy strikes.

This was the case for Mary Mrozowski, who has been called the "founding genius" behind the Welcoming Prayer. I keep her inspirational story close to my heart and think of her as a kindred spirit, as I have learned this prayer form and used it often. Mrozowski was a founding member of Chrysalis House, a contemplative community located in Warwick, New York, and she was also one of the founding members of Contemplative Outreach. The Welcoming Prayer emerged from her interactions in the 1980s with Father Thomas Keating, his teachings, and her own experience of spiritual transformation.[12]

Mrozowski explained her spirituality this way: "To welcome and to let go is one of the most radically loving, faith-filled gestures we can make in each moment of each day. It is an open-hearted embrace of all that is in ourselves and in the world."[13] The Welcoming Prayer is, in Cynthia Bourgeault's words, "a powerful path for connecting the inner consent of Centering Prayer with the outer requirement of unconditional presence [or surrender] in daily life."[14]

Never did Mrozowski realize that one day she would put the Welcoming Prayer to the ultimate test. On a crowded sidewalk one spring day, a reckless driver ran into her, and she was pinned to a wall. In the middle of the shock and pain, Mrozowski prayed out loud, "Welcome, pain. Welcome, pain. Welcome, pain. I let go of my desire to change the pain." Her equanimity astonished panicky onlookers, and in the moment, this helped gather more composure for everyone during the disastrous situation. She eventually healed from the accident.

I find the Welcoming Prayer often discharges my fear and helps me lay aside anxious concerns. It is the most challenging to do in the midst of betrayal, relational hardships, or abandonment—all of which signal areas of core wounding for me. During such circumstances, it's hard to really say the words and actually mean them. It probably will offer you some other particular challenge. Having this internal stance of welcome, not to pain or suffering itself, but a hospitality to the unfolding of life without our typical anxiety to control it, can be at the ready and serve as a form of spiritual preparedness that serves as a shelter in the storm. Since the prayer so acutely reveals my core wounds, I consider this a secondary gift of grace.

Fire bogs are a reality that will emerge within and dot our inner landscapes. They may dry up sometimes, or they may enlarge as circumstances arise. God is near in our suffering. When fire and anguish are the only languages we know or when we run out of things to say in the middle of the bog, we can know that this may be the best time and way to pray—with no words, to hold silent vigil at the edge of waiting. We may draw into the silence and find God there, befriending us with stillness and presence, inviting us to endure, not giving us pat answers that won't help.

In the next chapter, we discuss deep listening and the social components to healing our wild lands within. Then we will look at how spiritual formation can spark and sustain our actions in the world. Be sure to connect and reconnect with others on this journey. We do this together. Your reading companions need you, and you need them. At this book's end, you will be invited to review all you've been learning along the way, and then we will create space for blessing.

Spiritual Practice: The Welcoming Prayer

The Welcoming Prayer involves integrating and noticing feelings, emotions, thoughts, sensations, commotions, and commentaries in the body. We welcome the Divine indwelling into what we sense as our bodies by *saying*, "Welcome." The prayer continues with a few "letting go" statements that facilitate relinquishment and inner calm.[15]

1. Begin by bringing your thinking mind down into the heart and body area. Notice and sink into the feelings, emotions, thoughts, sensations, commotions, and commentaries in your body.

2. Accept the Divine indwelling in what you are experiencing by simply saying, "Welcome."

3. Adopt an attitude of surrender by inwardly affirming the following and repeating, as long as you need to, this phrase or a similar one that suits your specific needs:

    "I welcome what is. I let go of the desire for security, affection, and control. I let go of the desire to change the situation."

9

AT HOME WITHIN

Grounding Ourselves in Divine Love

After Henri Nouwen encountered Rembrandt's painting *The Return of the Prodigal Son* in 1989, he began a nine-year odyssey of emotional and spiritual discovery. Nouwen reflected later that this journey culminated in greater intimacy with God and a self-acceptance and wholeness he never dreamed possible. Not only did Nouwen carefully study the painting; he used it in *visio divina*, or "sacred seeing"—that is, a slow, attentive, worshipful practice of viewing an image while inviting God into the viewing. He spent countless quiet hours in prayerful meditation on what it represented. Using the painting, he placed himself within the parable of the prodigal son once told by Jesus.

These times of contemplative prayer and this intrepid inner work reaped an abundant harvest for Nouwen, one that many readers benefit from so many years later. In four years, he wrote eleven books. During those years, Nouwen dug deeply into his inner landscape and shared his findings—sometimes even while plunging into heartbreak, breakdown, and severe depression.

Nouwen was intently drawn to the figure of the shabby returning son in the painting, who is held in full embrace by the gracious father figure. Nouwen's core wound of esteem and affection was an ever-present and deep chasm in his life, and he regularly wrote about how he longed to feel accepted and loved by God. He explored his inner world and recognized how much he felt alienated from his biological father and, consequently, from God as a loving father. Over time, the continual stormy weather of Nouwen's inner climate shifted and improved as this area began to heal.

Next, he found himself identifying with the tense older brother in the painting. He challenged the difficult parts within himself that were holding onto resentment, anger, a sense of injustice, and competitiveness. He discovered that he was able to find God's grace to mend the wounds that created those recurring issues, repent of them, and find enriched ways of relating.

Lastly, he was coaxed to put himself in the place of the loving father figure in the painting. From that vantage point, he could receive the prodigal son aspects of himself with kindness so that he could also, in turn, act as a more spiritually mature guide toward others in his vocation as priest. Through prayer of the heart and by allowing God to cultivate the ground in the wounded and shadowy places within, Nouwen wrote the book *The Return of the Prodigal Son: A Story of Homecoming.* He authored thirty-eight other books in his life of just sixty-four years.[1] As Nouwen found, a brave exploration of our intimidating inner terrains can lead to the most fulfilling and fruitful years of our lives.

As we gaze around at our lands within now, we understand that we aren't so much taming the places and creatures of our inner worlds as we are cooperating and cocreating with the Spirit to cultivate, enjoy, and learn of all the beauty and mystery God makes for us there. Centered in Divine Love, we can handle the tough terrain and the tricky weather with more courage and preparedness than we could if we ran away from it or simply pretended it wasn't there. As we continue to discover and renovate the land through communion and intimacy with God in spiritual practices and are shepherded to the still waters, let's consider a few more aspects to soul care, relationships, and service that extend out from us and work among us.

Learning of Space and Grace

When we begin to notice what is within us, we often become aware of the largeness of this interior space. The space within is boundless! One who is familiar with this terrain and who has learned to abide in it feels freer to be themselves. Not only that, but they feel freer to liberate others by offering radical love and grace. Rather than putting expectations or timetables on others, those who know their own interior lives are able to accompany others on their unique relationships with and paths toward the Divine.

As our souls are nourished by silence and by setting time apart, we notice that our previous feelings of scarcity and lack dissipate. The stillness in our lives gradually seems more familiar and sustaining. Renewal takes hold. We begin to enjoy a greater sense of groundedness and well-being. This food of the soul becomes part of a normal, balanced, healthy diet we enjoy that makes overall life improve.

When we are soul-fed by regular periods of silence and solitude, we have more internal reserves to spare in service as well. Dr. Barbara A. Holmes writes, "Through acts of contemplation, individuals and congregations enter the liminal space where the impossible becomes possible."[2] This gives us more compassion and understanding for others and reservoirs from which to source empathy. We may find ourselves more able to listen to the people we once found bothersome. We may feel more caring for others. We may find outbursts of frustration and anger will be less frequent. Where someone might have easily lit the fast-acting incendiary devices of our rage, now we might find we have longer fuses. Best of all, for the greater good of the world, we may sense a more immediate kinship with others and be willing to help those in need. The blossoms of spiritual fruit!

Care of Soul

Let's be sure to keep our inner terrains tended and our bodies cared for. Self-care, which is a subset of soul care, builds up habits that produce resilience. In this way, we are primed to undergo situations that require perseverance. If we remember to regularly and honestly check in with ourselves to see if all is well with our physical bodies, which are part of our whole souls, we practice another kind of "soul hygiene" for overall wellness. As integrated beings, our bodily lives must be considered too. Eating nutritiously, sleeping enough, getting social and emotional support from others: there can be no more taking shortcuts or sloughing off as unimportant any of these things that make us well.

Let us stay grounded in the mysterious, intimate contemplative practices that bind us closely to our loving Creator. We can make them part of routine habits and rhythms of how we live. My hope is that long after you finish this book, you will take these spiritual practices that you've tried and make them regular parts of your day.

"Contemplation plugs [us] into the catalytic center of God's Spirit, into the divine power that permeates every aspect of life," writes Rev. Holmes.[3] As we make nourishing contemplative practices and caretaking of our inner worlds part of our regular schedules, we thrive like plants that are properly cultivated and watered.

The practice of checking in with ourselves—regularly noticing how we feel—actually rewires our brains. This practice helps us reach a more thorough and regularly attuned form of consciousness and sensing. And a more neurologically integrated brain is more resilient. We must train ourselves to feel the sensations of our bodies and incorporate ways to keep track of these sensations. Trauma and suffering can habituate us to numbing the sensations of our bodies. Dr. Bessel A. van der Kolk writes, "The bodies of child-abuse victims are tense and defensive until they find a way to relax and feel safe. In order to change, people need to become aware of their sensations and the way that their bodies interact with the world around them. Physical self-awareness is the first step in releasing the tyranny of the past."[4]

As we check in with ourselves, we will likely notice better self-regulation of our emotions, better sleep, and enhanced mood. People who begin to include intentional spaces of inner silence or meditation in their days commonly report these changes. Change is noticed in as soon as a week or two, and sometimes much sooner. Schedule appointments every day to check in with yourself and to gather the graces of your life into one piece.

Inviting Deep Listening

One of the simplest and most direct ways to tap into the still center of ourselves is through the embodied act of deep listening. We can listen deeply to ourselves, and to others, and to God. Parker J. Palmer speaks to this out of the influence of his Quaker tradition. The key ingredient to this kind of listening practice is the infusion of nonviolence. Because of their nonviolent stance, Quakers focus on invitation, not compulsion or coercion, in their ways of being and interacting. Invitation can open up to us deeper ways of knowing ourselves and others.

Deep listening to ourselves, to others, and to the "Inward Light" (as Quakers often refer to the Divine) involves a thorough form of hospitality few of us have encountered. For instance, one responds to the prompting invitation of the Inward Light as it influences one's conscience during a Society of Friends meeting. Any who gather for a Quaker meeting are invited to speak at a prompting from the Spirit, no matter their role. People participate in Quaker meetings without any liturgy or schedule.

Palmer designed his leadership and development materials at the Center of Courage and Renewal with the same approach of nonviolence. For instance, educators and leaders who gather for trainings are invited—not pressured or expected—to share an insight during a group time called Circle of Trust. In these circles, listening is an act of hospitality toward oneself and others; "being with" is an opportunity for greater understanding and deeper ways of knowing. From a place of safety, one is invited into greater depths when they sense they are ready.[5]

Community support doesn't refer to therapeutic advice or directing someone on what to do. From Palmer's vantage point, when an issue is soul-deep, the soul alone knows how to find a pathway by engaging with the terrain itself. Befriending the ways of stillness, silence, and listening draws us into deeper and deeper speech. Learning, noticing, and healing are simpler to find from a place of deep listening.

Palmer emphasizes guiding principles that are enacted in the Circle of Trust groups: each person yearns to have their perspective honored and acknowledged. No one desires to be a "project"—someone to be saved, advised, corrected, or fixed with clever ideas or suggestions. To make a person an object of our aims or ambitions, even righteous ones, is to do a kind of violence to their volition and human dignity. "Relational trust is built on movements of the human heart such as empathy, commitment, compassion, patience, and the capacity to forgive," says Palmer.[6]

Be a good listener. Palmer advises us to restrain ourselves and our desires to impose our will, to tell our stories, or to instruct when we are part of a community in conversation. When we hold space for someone (even ourselves), we listen deeply, without judgment and without offering criticism or advice. Then the truth can surface for itself and we can truly allow another person—or ourselves—to be seen and heard. Only at this point of engaged and innocuous presence—deep listening—with others will the wild animal of one's soul not be frightened back into the forest. This is also how we befriend ourselves and others in new ways and find greater wholeness. John O'Donohue wrote of this kind of listening and acceptance beautifully: "When you learn to love and let yourself be loved, you come home to the hearth of your own spirit. You are warm and sheltered. You are completely at one in the house of your own longing and belonging."[7]

Finding Social Support

Social support is not the same as proximity to others or chatting with a friend. Being truly heard and seen by the people around us and feeling that we are held in someone else's mind and heart run much deeper than ordinary conversation. It also requires reciprocity, in which the wealth of support is *shared*. This is the kind of social support that brings true transformation and healing.

For our physiology to calm down, heal, and reintegrate, we need a visceral feeling of safety. No doctor can write a prescription for friendship and love, where these feelings may be created and sustained. These are complex and hard-earned capacities. We may need to start small, one confidante at a time over a long time—years.

Finding friends or professionals we can trust to help with our mutual healing processes is critical. Trauma happens within the context of relationships and communities, and our healing needs to emerge from communities and relationships too. In these places, we must find safe and healthy ways to build trust, process pain, and gain new ground among and through social contexts.

Sharing with others what you fear and your process through the fire bogs or shadowy lands empowers others tremendously. We need to find a fitting group to support us and in which we can support others. Sharing also gives you even more courage to continue the journey through the wild land within. When you share your experiences—of using the interior space for centering down, for example, or of the way that solitude exposed locked-away fears and pain—you will find that others may have had similar experiences. Not only that, but many people will express how grateful they are that you have shared so vulnerably.

How good to give a testimony about the ground we've covered! When we witness the pain in ourselves and in each other, we heal together. Sharing gives us all more determination. It inspires others to explore their own tricky grounds. Courage is what we have in the presence (not the absence) of our fears. Though we usually don't realize it at the time, fear always presents a fiercer visage than is really there.

Rooting Action in Spiritual Formation

Our journeys into our flyover countries—our wilderness within—can never be merely about our own personal renewal or healing. We are each a wild land among many. Facilitating the restoration in our relationships and in our connections and networks is how we begin the greater work of healing. Each person from the inside out and our society at large must move toward these purposes. It gives us an extraordinary sense of meaning and gladness to be a part of God's ongoing and infinite restorative work of shalom. Nouwen underscores this relationship of inner healing and outer action well: "Christian life is not a life divided between times for action and times for contemplation. No. Real social action is a way of contemplation, and real contemplation is the core of social action."[8]

Being grounded spiritually is how we build resolve and resilience for compassionate action. It gives us ongoing strength for putting things right in our surroundings and the greater world. As we become more transparent and more rooted in God's love, we can band with others and begin the long haul toward restoration, reconciliation, and justice in our communities and the greater world.

I find a beautiful example of how to be firmly rooted in spiritual practices and work tirelessly for justice in the lives of the intrepid Americans involved in the civil rights movement in the mid-twentieth century. These leaders guided us toward a deeply spiritual way of being in the world. This fueled their active resistance toward violence and sustained them to carry on to long-awaited freedoms and hoped-for victories. In his first book, *Stride toward Freedom*, Dr. Martin Luther King Jr. illuminated six principles that undergird his philosophy of nonviolence. These principles point to both an ideology of change *and* a grounded spirituality:

1. Nonviolence is not passive but requires courage;
2. Nonviolence seeks reconciliation, not defeat of an adversary;
3. Nonviolent action is directed at eliminating evil, not destroying an evil-doer;

4. A willingness to accept suffering for the cause, if necessary, but never to inflict it;
5. A rejection of hatred, animosity or violence of the spirit, as well as refusal to commit physical violence;
6. Faith that justice will prevail.[9]

These principles stand as righteous pillars of defiance against cruelty and injustice. They are seeded with a boldness and fortitude sourced in a deeper reality. Dr. King clarifies that the preparation for this kind of work is self-purification. This is composed of "the cleansing of anger, selfishness, and violent attitudes of the heart and soul."[10] This is indeed the cultivation of places in the land within.

Because of his commitment to eradicating second-class status for Blacks, Rev. Fred Shuttlesworth, founder the Alabama Christian Movement for Human Rights, stated, "We appeal to the citizenry of Birmingham, Negro and white, to join us in this witness for decency, morality, self-respect, and human dignity." This organization collaborated with other groups in the movement to desegregate public facilities and to attain equal employment opportunities for the Black citizens of Birmingham. Their actions created a heightened national awareness of the rampant police brutality in Birmingham and the need for further protection for the human rights of Black Americans and contributed to the passage of the 1964 Civil Rights Act. Beyond being effective in specific cases of injustice, the organization was centered on nurturing the spiritual fruit that could power and sustain those striving together. A life rich in contemplative practices and selflessness was a prerequisite to become involved.

The Alabama Christian Movement for Human Rights organization had everyone agree to the group's commandments and sign a pledge on a commitment card they would always carry with them.[11] Before coming to demonstrations or even helping out in practical ways—listed on the card were tasks including "Run errands," "Drive my car," "Fix food for volunteers," "Clerical work," "Make phone calls," "Answer phones," "Mimeograph," "Type," "Print signs," "Distribute leaflets"— those interested had to sign a pledge. By signing, they were promising to do ten practices. The card read this way:

I hereby pledge myself—my person and body—to the nonviolent movement. Therefore, I will keep the following ten commandments:

1. Meditate daily on the teachings and life of Jesus.
2. Remember always that the non-violent movement seeks in Birmingham justice and reconciliation—not victory.
3. Walk and talk in the manner of love, for God is love.
4. Pray daily to be used by God in order that all [people] might be free.
5. Sacrifice personal wishes in order that all [people] might be free.
6. Observe with both friend and foe the ordinary rules of courtesy.
7. Seek to perform regular service for others and for the world.
8. Refrain from the violence of fist, tongue, or heart.
9. Strive to be in good spiritual and bodily health.

10. Follow the directions of the movement and of the captain on a demonstration.

This commitment card helped bulwark the integrated lives of those willing to sacrifice their very bodies for freedom. They didn't just believe in nonviolence; they literally became nonviolence. This embodiment is the lesson. Our involvement with others and for the greater good and healing in the world must be grounded firmly in our spiritual formation and sourced in Divine Love. For our Black brothers and sisters and others involved at the time, this transformation first took place in inner landscapes laden with the fruit of the Spirit. The teachings of Jesus Christ and our abiding in him in the Spirit sustain us for the work and the difficulties ahead.

Bless This Land

In many ways, we have just begun to explore the wild land within. I'm excited to continue with you. Review the ground you've covered by going through your notes and this book, which should serve you as a kind of ongoing reference guide. Find more companions along the way, and go back to places in the book that need to be reinforced in your mind. Reach out and help others so they can be brave on their journeys into flyover country as well.

Please make regular trips to your inner landscape—multiple times a day. Check on the animals; notice the weather; get a feel for the climate shifts; and work to make gardens, forests, and orchards by allowing God to seed the land. Ready the land there in every season with contemplative practices you've already learned and helpful additional practices you find on the way. Invite God's light into the chasms or fire bogs that give you trouble so that those places are illuminated and made whole. Go onward in peace, and be courageous in this everlasting journey. The presence of God is with you always.

Spiritual Practice: Recollecting and Revisiting

Revisit the responses to the Quaker queries you've encountered along the way. Consider how your attitudes have shifted and what you have learned. Then ask yourself one or two of the queries that are most meaningful to you. Write down your new and updated responses. If you can share this progress in a discussion with someone else or with a small group, it will be most beneficial. Discuss any surprises or insights you found as you've learned more. I would be so happy to hear from you.

I leave you with a blessing. A blessing is a sincere and kind bidding of goodness for another and for the better to become true. To get a blessing requires no special action to perform or fancy words to say. All you have to do is receive it. Blessings are at our disposal to offer up at any time for anyone.

Blessings set into motion our desires for goodness and for the life we envision with the Divine Sower. There is a greater story happening around and within us all, and saying a blessing means we concede to make ourselves ground for that greater story.

Receive this blessing:

Enter into the infinite kingdom. It is the land within you. It extends from your core and out into the world and among you and all others. May the seeds of the Spirit's fruit find purchase among fertile soil, ready for God's loving work. May what springs up sprout in joy and be so lovely that you wouldn't have dared to dream it—but at long last, all is well and lush. May your deepest places be met with the patience of your own grace to yourself and with the kindness of God's light. May you extend the love overflowing from your healed places to make gentle the path for someone else and extend a hand for the next person who may be wearier than you know. Know from your deepest place within that you are loved. May the presence of the Divine—the Source of Love—fill your senses with tender embrace, mercies, and homecoming. May it be well with your soul. Amen.

ACKNOWLEDGMENTS

This book feels a long time coming, and there are many relationships that have played a part in helping me—too numerous to list here. Most of all, to the people at 1517 Media; Broadleaf Books; and my kind, intrepid, and skillful editor, Valerie Weaver-Zercher—I feel saturated with gratitude and very blessed to bring this book to life with you. Thank you to my friends who helped along the way: Parker J. Palmer, Carl McColman, Rachel Reyes, Jon M. Sweeney, Casey Tygrett, Sheridan Voysey, Ed Cyzewski, Andō, Charlotte Donlon, David Dark, Ines McBryde, Robert Monson, Cassidy Hall, Nicole Walters, Karen Gonzales, Marlena Graves, Khristi Adams, Terrence Lester, Marc Thomas Shaw, Phuc Luu, Noel Young, Dan White Jr., Michelle Williams, Jessica Whittemore, Molly Steranko, Lisa Deam, Pam Jaskierski, all of my wonderful Patreon supporters, and the many writers and friends who have encouraged me. Thank you.

RESOURCES

This short list may guide you to find companions or aid in consistency with spiritual practices as you continue to journey in your wild land within. Keep adding to the list as you find more helpful places, people, and resources.

Spiritual Direction

Find a list of spiritual directors at SDIworld.org.

Websites

My websites: lisadelay.com | patreon.com/sparkmymuse

ContemplativeOutreach.org

ContemplativeMind.org

Abbeyofthearts.com

acontemplativepath-wccm.org (the World Community for Christian Meditation)

Books

Adele Ahlberg Calhoun, *Spiritual Discipline Handbook*

Barbara A. Holmes, *Joy Unspeakable:*
Contemplative Practices of the Black Church

Christine Valters Paintner, *The Soul's Slow Ripening*

Parker J. Palmer, *A Hidden Wholeness:*
The Journey toward an Undivided Life

Spiritual Practice Apps

Pray as You Go

Lectio 365

Centering Prayer (from Contemplative Outreach)

Podcasts

Spark My Muse

On Being

Encountering Silence

NOTES

Chapter 1

1 John O'Donohue, *Eternal Echoes: Celtic Reflections on Our Yearning to Belong* (New York: Harper Perennial, 2000), 5.

Chapter 2

1 "Sayings of St. Anthony the Great," St. Mary and St. Antonious Coptic Orthodox Church, accessed May 16, 2020, https://tinyurl.com/ydhyt4wg.

2 Richard Finn, *Asceticism in the Graeco-Roman World* (Cambridge: Cambridge University Press, 2009), 94.

3 Vladimir Lossky, *The Mystical Theology of the Eastern Church* (New York: St. Vladimir's Seminary Press, 1976), 127.

4 Christianity first occurred as an offshoot of Judaism by Jewish people in places in and near Jerusalem. These were not places that had much Hellenistic or Roman cultural influence on their religious expressions. Christianity maintained largely Jewish—that is, Eastern and nonempire—ways of practice and understanding for many decades. In 70 CE, the first Christians fled Jerusalem after it was sacked and destroyed by the Roman Empire. Christian centers started to take

shape in other places like Antioch, Alexandria, Asia Minor, Caesarea, Cyprus, Thrace, and Libya. Christians also settled in many places in the East, Near East, Middle East, and West.

5 Kenneth Wilson, *Augustine's Conversion from Traditional Free Choice to "Non-free Free Will": A Comprehensive Methodology* (Tübingen, Germany: Mohr Siebeck, 2018), 16–18, 157–187.

6 Catholic Church, "Catechism of the Catholic Church," The Seven Sacraments of the Church, November 2019, https://tinyurl.com/ykqqof.

7 Paraphrasing and notes from Rev. Angela Tilby in "Evagrius of Pontus and the Transformation of the Passions," video, June 1, 2014, fifth in a series of Thursday lunchtime talks at St. Giles' Church, Oxford, on exploring the wisdom of the mystics, from May 1, 2014, to June 19, 2014, https://youtu.be/UF7SmAHuAbo.

8 John Chryssavgis, "Repentance and Confession: Introduction," Greek Orthodox Archdiocese of America, accessed May 15, 2020, https://tinyurl.com/yb4hauzm.

9 Ibid.

10 Bessel A. van der Kolk, *The Body Keeps the Score: Brain, Mind, and Body in the Healing of Trauma* (New York: Penguin, 2014), 102.

Chapter 3

1 Stuart Banner, *How the Indians Lost Their Land: Law and Power on the Frontier* (Cambridge, MA: Belknap, 2007), 171.

2 Eric Kades, *The Dark Side of Efficiency: Johnson v. M'Intosh and the Expropriation of American Indian Lands* (Philadelphia: University of Pennsylvania Press, 2000), 148.

3 Tinker purposefully does not capitalize Euro and Christian so as to not normalize the atrocities that have occurred. George Tinker, "Redskin,

Tanned Hide: A Book of Christian History Bound in the Flayed Skin of an American Indian: The Colonial Romance, Christian Denial and the Cleansing of a Christian School of Theology," *Journal of Race, Ethnicity, and Religion* 5, no. 9 (October 2014): 3, https://tinyurl.com/y5febvx4.

4 Ibid., 7–9.

5 Elise Hansen, "The Forgotten Minority in Police Shootings," CNN (online), November 13, 2017, https://tinyurl.com/ycuf3afr.

6 Nikki Tundel, "American Indians Balance Native Customs with Christianity," MPR News, November 14, 2013, https://tinyurl.com/y89h5a3s.

7 Barbara A. Holmes, *Joy Unspeakable: Contemplative Practices of the Black Church*, 2nd ed. (Minneapolis: Fortress, 2017), 2–22.

8 Ibram Kendi, *Stamped from the Beginning: The Definitive History of Racist Ideas in America* (New York: Hachette, 2017), 23.

9 "Pope Nicholas V and the Portuguese Slave Trade," African Laborers for a New Empire: Iberia, Slavery, and the Atlantic World, Lowcountry Digital History Initiative, accessed June 14, 2020, https://tinyurl.com/yakm7zeo.

10 The Geospatial and Statistical Data Center allows viewers to comb census data over time. Geospatial and Statistical Data Center, "Historical Census Browser," University of Virginia Library, accessed May 20, 2020, https://tinyurl.com/ya9jzmfj.

11 James H. Cone, *The Cross and the Lynching Tree* (Maryknoll, NY: Orbis, 2011), Kindle.

12 Ibid.

13 Wilda C. Gafney, *Womanist Midrash: A Reintroduction to the Women of the Torah and the Throne* (Louisville: Westminster John Knox, 2017), Kindle.

14 Ibid.

15 Igartúa v. Trump, 868 F.3d 24 (1st Cir. 2017), accessed August 13, 2020, https://tinyurl.com/y4ruwera.

16 Maureen Campesino, Michael Belyea, and Gary Schwartz, "Spirituality and Cultural Identification among Latino and Non-Latino College Students," *Hispanic Health Care International* 7, no. 2 (December 31, 2008), https://tinyurl.com/y78br4g7.

17 Ada Maria Isasi-Diaz, *La Lucha Continues: Mujerista Theology* (Maryknoll, NY: Orbis, 2004), 6.

18 Census Bureau in 2018, 21 million or 6.5 percent; US Census Bureau, "American Community Survey Demographic and Housing Estimates: ACS 5-Year Estimates Data Profiles," US Census Bureau, accessed June 22, 2020, p. 1, https://tinyurl.com/y75tfoze.

19 Daniel Hartnett, "Remembering the Poor: An Interview with Gustavo Gutiérrez," *America Magazine*, February 3, 2003, https://tinyurl.com/ubelxyy.

20 Ibid.

21 Phuc Luu, *Jesus of the East: Reclaiming the Gospel for the Wounded* (Harrisonburg, VA: Herald, 2020), 14, 18, 38, 119.

22 Holmes, *Joy Unspeakable*, 20.

Chapter 4

1 Bessel A. van der Kolk, *The Body Keeps the Score: Brain, Mind, and Body in the Healing of Trauma* (New York: Penguin, 2014), 98–99.

2 Ibid., 120.

3 John O'Donohue, *Anam Cara: A Book of Celtic Wisdom* (New York: HarperCollins, 2009), Kindle.

4 Cynthia Bourgeault, *Centering Prayer and Inner Awakening*, 1st ed. (Cambridge, MA: Cowley, 2004), 106.

5 Ibid., 107.

6 Lisa Feldman Barrett, *How Emotions Are Made* (New York: Mariner Books, 2018), 213.

7 Ibid., 57.

8 Van der Kolk, *Body Keeps the Score*, 99.

Chapter 5

1 Evagrius Ponticus, *The Praktikos and Chapters on Prayer*, vol. 4, trans. John Eudes Bamberger (Kalamazoo, MI: Cistercian, 1981), 4:14.

2 Michael Loungo, Stephen Tucker, and Claire Wilson, "Seven Deadly Sins and Seven Lively Virtues: A Lent Course for Churches Together in North Camden," Hampstead Parish Church, February 2014, p. 6, https://tinyurl.com/y7todagd.

3 Evagrius Ponticus, *The Praktikos and Chapters on Prayer*, vol. 4, trans. John Eudes Bamberger (Kalamazoo, MI: Cistercian, 1981), 4:14.

4 Cynthia Bourgeault, "Seven Sins, Eight Thoughts, Nine Types with Cynthia Bourgeault," Enneagram Global Summit, Hosted by Jessica Dibb with Cynthia Bourgeault, June 26, 2019, https://tinyurl.com/yyrgx039.

5 Ponticus, *Praktikos*, 4:11.

6 Ibid.

7 Ibid., 12.

8 Robin Darling Young, "Evagrius the Iconographer: Monastic Pedagogy in the Gnostikos," *Journal of Early Christian Studies* 9, no. 1 (Spring 2001): 53–71.

9 Bourgeault, "Seven Sins."

10 Thomas Keating, *Open Mind, Open Heart*, 20th anniversary ed. (New York: Continuum, 2008), 97.

11 Henri Nouwen, *The Way of the Heart: Connecting with God through Prayer, Wisdom, and Silence*, rev. ed. (New York: Ballantine, 2003), 49.

Chapter 6

1 Coptic Orthodox Diocese of the Midlands, UK, "If a Man Loves God . . . ," quote by St. Anthony the Great, accessed May 5, 2020, https://tinyurl.com/y7k79pft.

2 Carl McColman, "At the Edge of Waiting—a Celtic Approach to Contemplation," June 9, 2017, https://tinyurl.com/ybs69z26.

3 Thomas Merton, *The Asian Journal of Thomas Merton* (New York: New Directions, 1973), 308.

4 Evagrius Ponticus, *The Praktikos and Chapters on Prayer*, vol. 4, trans. John Eudes Bamberger (Kalamazoo, MI: Cistercian, 1981), 4:2.

5 Thomas Keating, *The Method of Centering Prayer: The Prayer of Consent* (Butler, NJ: Contemplative Outreach, 2016), 1–2.

6 Dionysius the Areopagite, *Dionysius the Areopagite, Works (1897)*, trans. John Parker (Grand Rapids, MI: Christian Classics Ethereal Library, n.d.), 11, 14–26, https://tinyurl.com/y2yye2tv.

7 Ibid.

8 Kallistos Ware, *Act Out of Stillness: The Influence of Fourteenth-Century Hesychasm on Byzantine and Slav Civilization*, ed. Daniel J. Sahas (Toronto: Hellenic Canadian Association of Constantinople and the Thessalonikean Society of Metro Toronto, 1995), 4.

9 Thomas Keating, *Invitation to Love: The Way of Christian Contemplation* (New York: Continuum, 2007), 110.

10 Marc Thomas Shaw, *Dante's Road: The Journey Home for the Modern Soul* (Vestal, NY: Anamchara Books, 2019), Kindle.

Chapter 7

1 Parker Palmer, *A Hidden Wholeness: The Journey toward an Undivided Life* (San Francisco: Jossey-Bass, 2004), 58.

2 Antoine de Saint-Exupéry, *The Little Prince* (New York: Harcourt Brace with Scholastic, 1971), 78–80, 83.

3 Ibid., 84, 88.

4 Carl McColman, "Eps 129—Carl McColman—Mysticism," interview show notes, *Spark My Muse*, accessed May 2, 2020, https://tinyurl.com/y76er6aa.

5 Henri J. M. Nouwen, *Reaching Out: The Three Movements of the Spiritual Life* (New York: Image/Doubleday, 1986), 74.

6 John O'Donohue, *Anam Cara: A Book of Celtic Wisdom* (New York: HarperCollins, 2009), Kindle.

Chapter 8

1 For more on this massacre, see Scott Ellsworth, "Tulsa Race Massacre," *The Encyclopedia of Oklahoma History and Culture*, Oklahoma Historical Society, 2009; online ed., accessed April 10, 2020, https://www.okhistory.org/publications/enc/entry.php?entry=TU013.

2 Scott Ellsworth, *Death in a Promised Land: The Tulsa Race Riot of 1921* (Baton Rouge: Louisiana State University Press, 1992), 72.

3 Peter A. Levine, "Basic Principles and Concepts of Somatic Experiencing," accessed May 20, 2020, https://tinyurl.com/ybffys37.

4 Bessel A. van der Kolk, *The Body Keeps the Score: Brain, Mind, and Body in the Healing of Trauma* (New York: Penguin, 2014), 65.

5 John O'Donohue, *Anam Cara: A Book of Celtic Wisdom* (New York: HarperCollins, 2009), Kindle.

6 James H. Cone, *The Cross and the Lynching Tree* (Maryknoll, NY: Orbis, 2011), 158, Kindle.

7 Bessel A. van der Kolk, *The Body Keeps the Score: Brain, Mind, and Body in the Healing of Trauma* (New York: Penguin, 2014), Kindle.

8 Annie Dillard, *Teaching a Stone to Talk* (New York: HarperCollins, 1982), 94–95.

9 "Sitting Shiva," Shiva.com, accessed June 5, 2020, https://tinyurl.com/y7mrv7ms.

10 "A Conversation with Kathleen Norris," Spirituality and Practice, accessed May 18, 2020, https://tinyurl.com/ybxn30g3.

11 Cone, *Cross and the Lynching Tree*, 106.

12 We can also draw parallels between this prayer form (Welcoming Prayer) and the seventeenth-century spiritual classic *Abandonment to Divine Providence* by Jean-Pierre de Caussade.

13 Mary Mrozowski (website), accessed April 20, 2020, https://www.marymrozowski.com.

14 Cynthia Bourgeault, *Centering Prayer and Inner Awakening* (Cambridge, MA: Cowley, 2004), 140.

15 Mary Mrozowski (website).

Chapter 9

1 Various details gathered from Nouwen's founding archivist's work. Gabrielle Earnshaw, *Henri Nouwen and the Return of the Prodigal Son: The Making of a Spiritual Classic* (Orleans, MA: Paraclete, 2020).

2 Barbara A. Holmes, *Joy Unspeakable: Contemplative Practices of the Black Church*, 2nd ed. (Minneapolis: Fortress, 2017), 20.

3 Ibid.

4 Bessel A. van der Kolk, *The Body Keeps the Score: Brain, Mind, and Body in the Healing of Trauma* (New York: Penguin, 2014), 102.

5 Parker Palmer, *A Hidden Wholeness: The Journey toward an Undivided Life* (San Francisco: Jossey-Bass, 2004), 83.

6 Ali Schultz, "Building Relational Trust: Reboot Podcast with Parker J. Palmer," Center for Courage & Renewal, June 13, 2016, https://tinyurl.com/ybk38ody.

7 John O'Donohue, *Anam Cara: A Book of Celtic Wisdom* (New York: HarperCollins, 2009), Kindle.

8 Henri Nouwen, *Creative Ministry* (New York: Doubleday, 1991), 88.

9 Martin Luther King Jr., *Stride toward Freedom* (Boston: Beacon, 2010), 84–88.

10 Ibid.

11 Copy of an original card found at "Martin Luther King, Jr.," WallBuilders, January 2, 2017, https://tinyurl.com/yd7p9keo; "Nonviolence Pledge," Bhamwiki, last modified January 25, 2018, 12:59, https://tinyurl.com/y82mfj2c.